START YOUR

NEW LIFE

TODAY

START YOUR NEW LIFE TODAY

An Exciting New Beginning with God

JOYCE MEYER

hachette INDIA

This paperback edition published in 2012 by Hachette India 612/614, 6th floor, Time Tower, M.G. Road, Sector 28, Gurgaon 122001 India under arrange ment and licence from Faith Words, Hachette Book Group USA, 237 Park Avenue, New York, NY 10017

Printed and bound in India by Manipal Technologies Limited, Manipal

First Edition : April 2012

SRD

MIX
Paper from responsible sources
FSC™ C043100

Contents

PART ONE
A BRAND-NEW START

PART TWO
YOU ARE SPIRIT, SOUL, AND BODY

PART ONE

A BRAND-NEW START

INTRODUCTION

The Most Important Decision You Will Ever Make

Do you sometimes wish you could start over? Or do you lead a successful life from all outward appearances but often wonder, *Surely there must be more to life than this*? In either case, there is good news for you. God wants to make your life new. He wants to give you a brand-new start if you need one.

Some people have tried religion hoping to find a solution to their frustrating existence. The people who find "religion" to be a burden of lifeless and unreasonable rules they are unable to keep have not found God. If you are one of those people, God has a new life to give you through His Son Jesus Christ. Jesus did not die to offer us religion, rather he died to give us an opportunity to have an intimate relationship with God through faith in Him.

If you need to feel loved, if you need your sins forgiven, if you need a friend who will help you with everything you do, if you need a great future, Jesus Christ is your answer. He is waiting to make you into a brand-new creation and give you a new life beyond the best you could possibly imagine.

If you are not satisfied with your life, then you must change something. Like anyone else, if you keep doing the same things you have always done, you will have the life you have always had. You need to make a decision, the most important decision you will ever make.

This decision is more important than your career choice, where you will attend college, whom you will marry, how you will invest your money, or where you will live. This decision concerns eternity. Eternity is time without end, and there is life after death. When we die, we don't cease to exist; we just begin to exist in another place. It has been said that dying is like going through a revolving door. We simply leave one place and go to another. We—every one of us—need to know where we will spend eternity.

The decision to receive Jesus is a new birth into a relationship with God for eternity beginning here on earth. When you receive Jesus as your Savior, your spirit is made alive to God. The Bible tells us if any man be in Christ, he is a new creature—re-created, born anew. Old things have passed away and all things are brand-new (see 2 Corinthians 5:17). Jesus takes our sin, and we are made right with God (see 2 Corinthians 5:21). God imputes righteousness to us or credits it to our account (see Romans 4:11).

The *new birth* happens in an instant. The burden of sin is lifted and we have a brand-new opportunity in our lives. Learning to live the new *life* is a process, but not one of trying to conform our behavior to a set of rules of what we think a Christian should be. Many Christians without an understanding of the new life God makes available to them through Jesus spend their lives trying to earn their own righteousness through doing good works. This doesn't work because God has already made them acceptable to Him at new birth through Jesus. Righteousness is a free gift from God to be received through faith. Trying to earn a free gift is like trying to get into a chair in which you are already sitting. It is impossible and very frustrating!

The new life is a process of transformation. God doesn't work just with our behavior; He also changes our hearts. When we seriously commit ourselves to Jesus as Savior and Lord, God begins transforming us from the inside out. He makes us like Jesus inside and wants to work what is in us *out* for other people to see and experience Jesus.

This transformation doesn't happen overnight and will seem very slow at times. One of the benefits of living in a relationship with

Jesus is the freedom to forget the past and move ahead into what God has for us. Jeremiah 29:11 describes the type of future He has in store for us: "For I know the thoughts and plans that I have for you, says the Lord, thoughts and plans for welfare and peace and not for evil, to give you hope in your final outcome."

When you are tempted to condemn yourself over the progress you think you should be making, turn your focus back on Jesus and God's promises for us recorded in the Bible. Remind yourself, "I'm okay and I'm on my way!" Remember that through faith you have been made right with God, and even though you have not arrived at perfection you are making progress.

Is it hard to make daily the right decisions to allow God to transform you? Yes, like many other things in life, it is hard at times, and we all make mistakes along the way. Is it worth sticking to? Absolutely!

Many people come to Jesus sincerely desiring to start a new life but don't know what to do after they receive Him. Take this opportunity to begin enjoying the journey God has for you, and start your new life today. You can have a dynamic intimate relationship with God and an amazing life!

CHAPTER 1

Start Your New Life Today

When you receive Jesus as your Savior, a divine exchange takes place. You give Him your sin and guilt, your shame and blame; He gives you right standing with God. You give Him the impoverished areas of your life; He gives you abundance. Jesus wants to give you beauty for ashes in every area of your life.

Sometimes people ask, "What would I have to give up if I became a Christian?"

I tell them, "Well, you would have to give up misery and sin. You would give up depression and discouragement, fear, worry, and anxiety. Do you carry around a burden of guilt and condemnation? You would also give that up."

Some people seem to think God wants to steal everything we enjoy. God isn't mean! He is love, and He is good. The Bible says God gives us all things ceaselessly to enjoy (see 1 Timothy 6:17). God loves us so much He sent His Son, Jesus, to earth to take our sins and give us life, life more abundantly (see John 3:16; 10:10). When we receive Jesus, we receive the kingdom of God within us, and that kingdom is righteousness, peace, and joy in the Holy Spirit (see Romans 14:17). We can choose to continue living with misery, depression, discouragement, fear, worry, anxiety, guilt, and condemnation, but Jesus wants us to receive freedom from those things. Through Jesus, "we are more than conquerors and gain a surpassing victory through Him Who loved us" (Romans 8:37).

A new birth into a new life is not supposed to be a door into a downtrodden, miserable existence of struggling to keep religious rules and regulations and feeling guilty when we fail. God gives us a new life and new desires to go along with it. We may lose interest in pursuing some things we used to like very much. A new life as a new creation in relationship with Jesus has brought the fulfillment we used to seek elsewhere. As these changes take place in us, we may not fully understand what we are feeling, but as we trust God He gives us clarity and we begin enjoying our new life in Christ.

The people who wonder what they would have to give up by choosing to receive Jesus are often cycling through repeated behaviors looking for fulfillment they will never find. If you are one of those people, are you tired of living the way you are living? Are you tired of going through life feeling bad about yourself all the time? Are you tired of making decisions you know are wrong and then feeling guilty about those decisions? Do you want to find the fulfillment you are missing? You may be tired of wondering what will happen to you in the future or tired of being afraid of dying. The good news is Jesus has peace for you.

If you haven't done a good job of running your own life, why not turn it over to the One who created you and knows more about you than you will ever know about yourself? If you start having trouble with an automobile, you take it back to the people who manufactured it to fix it. A similar principle is true with God. He created you and loves you very much. If your life is not satisfying to you, then take it to Him to fix it.

If you want to have a relationship with God here on earth and live with Him for eternity, you need to receive Jesus Christ as your Savior. We have all sinned and we all need a Savior. God sent His only Son to pay the penalty for our sins. He was crucified and shed His innocent blood as payment for our wrongdoing. He died and was buried, but on the third day He arose from the dead and is now seated in heaven, at the right hand of God the Father. He is your only hope of having peace, joy, and right standing with God.

Your life will not change unless you make that very important decision to receive Jesus as your Savior. The choice to accept new life in God is available to everyone. No one is left out. And no one can make your choice for you. It is yours and yours alone to make. What quality of life do you desire to have? Do you really want to follow the example you see in our society today? God's Word tells us we came into the world with nothing and we will go out with nothing (see 1 Timothy 6:7). Don't spend your life on things that will end up in a junkyard somewhere. Spend it laying up treasure in heaven (see Matthew 6:20).

> The choice to accept new life in God is available to everyone. No one is left out.

God is the Alpha and the Omega, the beginning and the end. In the beginning there was God and in the end there will be God. Every person will stand before Him and give an account of their life (see Romans 14:12). Do you want to use your life to build up treasures in heaven and let God use you in a way that can affect others for eternity? As you use your life for eternal significance, you will find the fulfilling life on earth you have been seeking. Anything we give to God immediately takes on immortality. If we give Him our time, talents, and possessions, He can use them to do good things here and for eternity. If we give them to the world, they will end up in a junkyard. It might be good for all of us to visit a junkyard once a year to remind ourselves that all temporal things eventually end up there.

CHAPTER 2

Leave Guilt Behind

Sin is deliberate disobedience to the known will of God. We have all sinned. There is no one on the earth who never sins (see Ecclesiastes 7:20). This is the bad news: "All have sinned and are falling short of the honor and glory which God bestows and receives" (Romans 3:23).

There is also good news. We can all be forgiven and made right with God: "[All] are justified and made upright and in right standing with God, freely and gratuitously by His grace (His unmerited favor and mercy) through the redemption which is [provided] in Christ Jesus" (v. 24).

Sin leads to destruction. God's Word says our sin will find us out (see Numbers 32:23). Sin brings a curse and obedience brings blessing (see Deuteronomy 28). For a season, people may appear to be unaffected by their sin. Their lives may appear to be as good as anyone else's, but in the end there will always be consequences for choices made. God speaks about the outcome of people attempting to live without Him: "And I will bring distress upon men, so that they shall walk like blind men, because they have sinned against the Lord; their blood shall be poured out like dust and their flesh like dung. Neither their silver nor their gold shall be able to deliver them in the day of the Lord's indignation and wrath. But the whole earth shall be consumed in the fire of His jealous wrath, for a full, yes, a sudden, end will He make of all the inhabitants of the earth" (Zephaniah 1:17–18).

These scriptures are fearsome, but they need not strike fear in the heart of a sincere believer in Jesus Christ. We who believe in Jesus shall never come up for judgment or condemnation (see John 3:18). God forgives our sins when we admit them, are sorry for them, and are willing to allow Him to help us turn entirely away from them.

"If we [freely] admit that we have sinned and confess our sins, He is faithful and just (true to His own nature and promises) and will forgive our sins [dismiss our lawlessness] and [continuously] cleanse us from all unrighteousness [everything not in conformity to His will in purpose, thought, and action]" (1 John 1:9). As new creations in right standing with God through Jesus, we have been provided the way to ask for and receive forgiveness and turn away from what we did wrong through the power of God's Spirit working in us.

The people who choose a life of sin rather than a life of obedience to God experience misery in their souls. Man lives in a body made of flesh and bones, but man is actually a spirit and has a soul. The soul is comprised of the mind, will, and emotions. The soul is the personality of man. No matter what people without Jesus do or possess, they cannot find anything to completely satisfy them. Sinners, in choosing to run their own lives instead of giving God control, suffer in their minds. When things don't go their way, they are in mental anguish and become frustrated or angry knowing nothing of the way of faith. To trust God—a power greater than themselves—is incomprehensible to them. They never allow rest to enter their minds—or their souls. Their lot in life is misery, misery, and more misery!

The constant companion of sinners is guilt. They are unable to escape it. They may try a variety of ways to ignore it, but deep down inside they know their lives are not right. The Bible is divided into two parts representing man's condition and God's solution to remove the sin and guilt separating man from Him. The first part, the Old Testament, is just that, the old way, representing the Old Covenant God used to cover the sins of the people until the time came for Jesus to establish a New Covenant.

Under the Old Covenant, the people's sins could be covered

through a system of giving sacrifices for their sins. The sins were covered but never removed. The guilt was always present. However, under the New Covenant—the second part of the Bible, the New Testament—Jesus became the perfect and final sacrifice. He didn't cover the sins but removed and completely washed them away, along with the guilt that accompanies them.

You need not wait for God to do something. He has already done what needs to be done. He gave His only Son to die in our place because only a perfect and sinless sacrifice could be offered to pay for our misdeeds. Justice has been satisfied and we can enjoy a life of freedom through believing in Jesus Christ and entering an intimate relationship with God through Him. We cannot go to God on our own—we need an advocate. We need someone as a go-between, and that someone is Jesus. In order to bring us to God, Jesus stood in the gap between us and God, the gap that our sin had created.

The only way to enter God's rest is through believing in Him (see Hebrews 4:3). Just as a child has his father in him (genetically), so God was in Christ reconciling the world back to Himself. God loves the people He created, and He is unwilling to see them live enslaved to sin without providing a way out. Jesus is the way!

God loves the people He created, and He is unwilling to see them live enslaved to sin without providing a way out. Jesus is the way!

Jesus has already paid for your sins. All you need to do is believe it and learn how to receive what He did and has for you to begin walking in your new life.

CHAPTER 3

You Are Free

When you become a new creation, Jesus removes your guilt. You may have already received Jesus and started your new life. Even though you know Jesus legally removed your guilt, do you still feel guilty?

God gave us emotions to enjoy, but they can also work against us and control our lives. Part of the process of learning how to allow God's Spirit to work in us to transform us is in learning how to manage our emotions. To do that we start by taking God's Word as the truth over the direction our emotions are trying to lead us. The way you learn the difference is through spending time reading, studying, and thinking about God's Word. As you do this "renewing of your mind" (see Romans 12:2), the power of God's Spirit, life, and truth in His Written Word works to transform you and your thinking. There is actually power inherent in the Word of God. As we take it into ourselves through reading, studying, or thinking about it, things actually change in us. Our mind changes, our emotions are calmed, and our wills are made pliable and willing to bend in God's direction.

Studying scriptures about freedom from guilt and condemnation will actually strengthen you and enable you to resist them when they come. Always remember there is power in the Word. Go to the concordance in the back of your Bible where you will find a list of scriptures by topic. Look up the scriptures you find on guilt and condemnation and write them down and read them out loud frequently. As you do this you are renewing your mind to think the way God thinks, and you will eventually enjoy complete freedom from the negative emotions of false guilt.

Believers in Jesus Christ don't have to spend their lives feeling guilty; and they don't have to sacrifice their peace and joy, because Jesus became a sacrifice once and for all and there is no sacrifice that ever needs to be added to His. Under the Old Covenant, the sacrifices had to be made over and over again, yet they never removed the guilt. Jesus became one sacrifice good for all time and it does remove the sin and guilt.

The guilt is legally removed, but we may still need to learn how to live free from the *feelings* of guilt. In the new life lived for Christ, we learn how to no longer allow our feelings to rule us. Spending the time to learn what the Word of God says gives us the knowledge to discern and live according to the truth. When we practice responding to situations we encounter in our daily lives with actions based on the truth of God's Word, we continue walking in the direction God has for us in our new life. Reacting with our emotions often takes us in a wrong direction. Learning the Word of God and obeying it no matter how we feel forms a lifestyle of obedience, ushering in blessings beyond compare. Instead of going through life reacting emotionally we can choose to act according to God's Word. We can examine each situation and choose to do what Jesus would do in that same situation. As we make right choices we will reap good consequences and our lives will be much more enjoyable.

Learning the Word of God and obeying it no matter how we feel forms a lifestyle of obedience, ushering in blessings beyond compare.

CHAPTER 4

Simply Receive God's Love for You

The story below illustrates the power of John 3:16 (KJV): "For God so loved the world that he gave his only begotten Son, that whosoever believeth in him should not perish, but have everlasting life."

In the city of Chicago, one cold, dark night, a blizzard was setting in. A little boy was selling newspapers on the corner. People were inside, out of the cold, and the little boy was so cold he really wasn't trying to sell many papers. He walked up to a policeman and said, "Mister, you wouldn't happen to know where a poor boy could find a warm place to sleep tonight, would you? You see, I sleep in a box, up around the corner there and down the alley, and it is awful cold. It sure would be nice to have a warm place to stay."

The policeman looked down at the little boy and said, "Well, I'll tell you what to do—you go down the street to that big white house and knock on the door. When they open the door, just say, 'John 3:16' and they will let you in."

So the boy did. He walked up the steps to the door and knocked, and a lady answered. He looked up and said, "John 3:16."

The lady said, "Come on in."

She took him in, sat him down in a split-bottom rocker in front of a great big fireplace and left. He sat there for a while and thought to himself, *John 3:16—I don't understand it, but it sure makes a cold boy warm.*

Later she came back and asked him, "Are you hungry?"

He said, "Well, just a little. I haven't eaten in a couple of days, and

I guess I could stand a little bit of food." The lady took him into the kitchen and sat him down at a table full of wonderful food, and he ate and ate until he couldn't eat anymore. Then he thought to himself, *John 3:16—I don't understand it, but it sure makes a hungry boy full.*

She took him upstairs to a bathroom with a huge bathtub filled with warm water. He sat there and soaked for a while. As he soaked, he thought to himself, *John 3:16—I don't understand it, but it sure makes a dirty boy clean.* The lady came in and got him, took him to a room, tucked him into an old feather bed, pulled the covers up around his neck, and kissed him good night. She turned out the lights. As he lay there in the darkness, he looked out the window and saw the snow coming down on that cold night. He thought to himself, *John 3:16—I don't understand it, but it sure makes a tired boy rested.*

The next morning she came up and took him down again to the same big table full of food. After he ate, she took him back to the same old split-bottom rocker in front of the fireplace. She got a Bible, sat down, and said, "Do you understand John 3:16?" "No, ma'am, I don't. The first time I ever heard it was last night when the policeman said to use it." She opened the Bible to John 3:16 and began to explain to him about Jesus. Right there in front of that fireplace, he gave his heart and life to Jesus. He sat there and thought, *John 3:16—I don't understand it, but it sure makes a lost boy feel safe.* (Author unknown)

> God loves us because He wants to, not because we deserve it.

Are you ready to receive the Father's love for you? It is a free gift and can only be received by faith. God loves us because He wants to, not because we deserve it. His love is unconditional and never ending. The Bible says it endures forever so we might as well receive it because it is not going to go away. If you have difficulty believing God loves you, begin confessing out loud that He does. You will eventually find that you really believe what you began saying by faith alone.

CHAPTER 5

Separate Your Who from Your Do

Sometimes we as Christians have the tendency to make things complicated. We may fall into trying to please God or win His love by doing good works or working our way into right standing with Him. Salvation is not based on what we do but on what Jesus did for us and whether we accept it.

Helping people, going to church on Sunday, giving offerings in church, refraining from saying bad words, being a nice person, and leading an all-around good life are good things to do. Will you go to heaven for doing such things? No.

The Bible says in order to enter the kingdom of heaven we must be born again (see John 3:3). It doesn't say in order to enter the kingdom of heaven we must attend church and do good works. This does not mean people should not go to church nor do good works. Yes, the Bible says for Christians to assemble together, and yes, the Bible shows us as our example Jesus going around doing good. The point is *doing* these things won't put us in the kingdom of heaven. We can't enter the kingdom of heaven based on what we do, but we do these things because we are part of God's kingdom. Our motivation is very important to God. He wants us to do what we do for Him out of a

We can't enter the kingdom of heaven based on what we do, but we do these things because we are part of God's kingdom.

heart of love and sincere desire. He does not want us to do them to get something from Him or to impress people.

The true work of the believer in Jesus Christ is to *believe*. It is the first thing we should be doing and is what makes us acceptable to Him. He also wants us to be assured of His love and never allow anything to separate us from it.

We need to know that God loves us! We need to know He loves us in the good times, and we need to know He loves us in the hard times. We need to know God loves us on the days we act right, and we need to know He loves us on the days we don't act so right. We need to know He loves us based not on what we do but on whom we have become in Christ. In other words, we have to know who we are and how to separate our "who" from our "do."

My children don't always do what I would like them to, but they are always my children and I never stop loving them. God has the same affection toward us and we should never doubt His love. Just as God corrects us, I correct my children to help them do better, but I will never, never, never stop loving them.

We won't *do* everything right all the time, but we are still in right standing with God through Christ. God still loves us every moment of the day. Does this mean we shouldn't take our sins seriously? As the apostle Paul said, "God forbid. How shall we, that are dead to sin, live any longer therein?" (Romans 6:2 KJV).

We take our sins seriously, and when we do things wrong, we ask for forgiveness and repent, turning from our sins by working with the Holy Spirit to continue making progress. We make mistakes. I make mistakes every day just like everybody else, but I thank God I don't live under guilt and condemnation anymore. As a Christian, I spent many years of my life living under a huge burden of guilt. God doesn't want us living under the burden of sin. He is the glory and the lifter of our heads (see Psalm 3:3). The Bible says among the blessings God has for us is to be the head and not the tail, above and not beneath (see Deuteronomy 28:13).

If you haven't surrendered your life to God by receiving His Son Jesus Christ as the only acceptable payment for your sins, are you ready to become a Christian? The Bible explains how to do this. In order to be saved from our sins, we must confess and acknowledge that Jesus is Lord, and we must believe in our hearts God raised Him from the dead: "Because if you acknowledge and confess with your lips that Jesus is Lord and in your heart believe (adhere to, trust in, and rely on the truth) that God raised Him from the dead, you will be saved" (Romans 10:9).

This type of believing is more than a mental acknowledgement; it is sincere and heartfelt. Many people believe there is a God, but they have not committed their lives to Him. God is the Author of life, and He wants you to willingly and gladly give back to Him the life He gave you. God created you with a free will, and He will not force you to choose Him. But whether or not you do will make the difference in your quality of life on earth and where you will spend eternity when you die.

To receive Jesus as your Savior, I encourage you to pray the following prayer aloud, listening to each of the words as you say them to be sure they have meaning to you personally:

Father God,
I come to You. I love You. Jesus, I believe in You. I believe You died for me. I believe You shed Your blood for me and paid the price for my sins.

I am a sinner and I am sorry for my sins. Forgive me for all of them. Jesus, I receive You now. Come and live in me and help me live my life the way You want me to live. I need a new beginning. Thank You for saving me. Now I ask You to teach me how to live for You. Jesus, I pray this in
Your name, amen.

It is a simple prayer. But if you prayed it with all your heart and really meant it, then it is a life-changing prayer.

If you are already a Christian but have been living under a sense of guilt and condemnation and you now realize you don't have to live that way, congratulations! You are about to begin enjoying your journey with God in a way that will be amazing. Don't ever let false guilt steal your joy again, because Jesus died so you could have and enjoy your life in abundance (see John 10:10).

CHAPTER 6

Rely on Truth Rather than Feelings

Feelings aren't always based on truth and they often change. When you accept Jesus as your Savior, you may feel peace or joy, relief or freedom, or you may feel nothing at all. If your prayer was sincere and heartfelt, be assured: God heard and answered your prayer. If your feelings tell you nothing happened, don't allow them to hold a position of dictator in your life. Believe in the truth of God's Word, not in your feelings. God is faithful and true to His promises, and He never changes.

Part of living the new life God has provided for you in Christ is learning not to live by your feelings. It is difficult for us at first because we have been accustomed to living by feelings all our lives. Feelings or emotions are part of the soul of man and they are neither good nor evil, but can be the root cause of both. Sometimes we enjoy our feelings and yet at other times they keep us from enjoying anything we do. Therefore, it is unwise to live by them. God invites us to live in the spirit where He dwells. We are to learn to be led by the spirit or the heart which is a deeper part of us. When I refer to the heart of man I am not referring to the physical organ called the heart; I am referring to the deepest part of us, the interior realm where God dwells.

You may not always feel God is with you on this wonderful journey in the new life He has for you, but His Word says He is always near. He is everywhere all the time, always watching over you. Some people try to hide things from God. This doesn't make sense because He knows everything! He may not approve of everything you do, but your position of right standing in Him through Jesus and His love for you never change. He approves of you and loves you and has provided forgiveness and cleansing for you, available for the asking. When you make a mistake, be quick to turn away from it and toward Him. Be quick to repent, ask Him for forgiveness, know He has forgiven you, and go on.

If you dwell on something you did by feeling guilty after asking for God's forgiveness, you are wasting your time. You are allowing feelings of guilt and condemnation to rise up to that position of dictator in your life to tell you to take on bondage from which Jesus freed you. If you ask God for forgiveness, but you don't feel forgiven, you can still be assured you are forgiven, because His Word says you are. God wants you to believe He forgave you, turn your attention back on enjoying and following Him, and press forward into the new life He has for you! God's Word is truth and we must exalt it above how we feel, what we think, what we want, what other people say, or what the devil says.

> God wants you to believe He forgave you, turn your attention back on enjoying and following Him, and press forward into the new life He has for you!

The Bible teaches us in Hebrews 4:12 that only the Word of God can divide soul and spirit. In other words, only God's Word, and nothing else, can tell me what truth really is. My soul can tell me what I think, but God's Word tells me what He thinks and I must choose to believe Him above everything else. If your own insight or understanding or feelings conflict with the truth of God's Word, choose to rely on the direction the truth of the Word is leading you.

Accepting the feelings of guilt and condemnation from which Jesus freed you is allowing accusations and lies from the devil to lead you. Jesus came to earth to destroy the works of the devil and free us to enjoy life to the full. The freedom and victory He purchased for us to accept and live by cost Him dearly.

We read and study the Word to know what it says, and we make a decision to receive and live in the freedom Jesus has for us. We make a decision to choose to believe the truth of God's Word over our own thoughts, feelings, and will and learn to continue choosing to do what we believe God wants us to do. We keep doing the right thing no matter how we feel. We do it on the good days when it is easy to do, on the bad days when we don't want to do it at all or ever, and on the mediocre days when we just go through the motions. We keep doing it until it becomes a lifestyle.

Our new way of living isn't merely a process of us conforming to some preconceived image we have of how to be a Christian, but a gradual transformation by the power of God's Spirit in us to become more like Jesus. God gives us the ability, the power, free for the asking, to do what needs to be done. The Christian life is about deepening our relationship with God through Jesus, receiving God's love, then loving one another. God provides the strength and ability for us to do anything He has asked of us. We have the privilege of leaning and relying on Him. Ask Him to help you because apart from Him you can do nothing (see John 15:5).

Jesus is the best friend you will ever have. Whether or not you feel He is there, He is there for you to depend on in every area of your life. Lean on and trust Him with all your heart and mind. He will take you in the right direction and make your paths straight. Talk to Him about everything. He always understands you and never rejects or condemns you. Nothing is too big for Him to handle, and for that matter, nothing is too small. No matter how you feel, you can always know to depend on God and the truth of His Word.

PART TWO

YOU ARE SPIRIT, SOUL, AND BODY

INTRODUCTION

The Way to a Happy Life

Jesus Christ has done a wonderful thing, and those of us who are born again (who receive Him as Savior and Lord) can receive and enjoy it through faith in Him. He has offered Himself to redeem our souls as well as our bodies and our spirits. In order to appropriate the full blessing Jesus purchased for us, we need to understand each of these three vital aspects of our being.

You are a tri-part being: You are a spirit, you have a soul, and you live in a body. Your spirit is the real you. When you make the decision to become a new creature in Christ, God's Holy Spirit comes to live in your spirit. Your spirit comes alive to God and wants to do what is good. When you and I look at other people, we see the physical body, but there is much more to a person than the physical body we see. The spiritual part is just as real. In fact, the Bible teaches us to live by the things of the spiritual realm, things we don't see. The only way to have a truly satisfying, happy life is to be led by the Holy Spirit.

Your soul is your mind, your will, and your emotions. Your soul's thoughts and wants and feelings don't necessarily agree with God's thoughts and desires. For example, no matter what kind of opinion you have of yourself, God's thoughts about you are so much better. We learn a new way of thinking, in line with God's thoughts, by reading and studying His Word. The Bible calls this process the renewing of the mind.

Your body is the house where your spirit and soul live while you are on earth. If you are a new creation, God also lives in that house!

The body has a mouth, and the mouth gives expression to the soul. In other words, the mouth tells everybody what you think and want and feel. It has great potential for causing trouble. The body's five physical senses—touch, smell, taste, sight, hearing—contribute to the way the soul thinks, what it wants, and how it feels. They may also lead us into trouble. Just think about what happens when people let their taste buds run their lives. Something we see with our eyes may affect our whole life. The Bible tells us not to walk by sight (see 2 Corinthians 5:7). In other words, we should learn to value unseen things in the spiritual realm more than the things we see with our physical eyes. At one point when the apostle Paul was undergoing tremendous trials and tribulations, he said he did not become discouraged because he looked not at the things which were seen but the things unseen (see 2 Corinthians 4:18). For example angels are all around us protecting us and yet we do not see them. God is with us at all times, but we don't see Him with our natural eye. God has a good plan for your life even though you may not feel at this moment that He does. Life gets exciting when we learn to see with the spiritual eye rather than merely the natural eye.

> We should learn to value unseen things in the spiritual realm more than the things we see with our physical eyes.

Your body tries to boss you around. The combination of the soul and body, "the flesh," fights the spirit to do as the soul wants. For example, on a Sunday morning when you wake up, your spirit may say, "Let's go to church!" but your body may say, "I don't want to get out of this bed." Some people may obey the body and go back to sleep; other people will follow the spirit and say, "Body, I don't care how you feel—we're going to church!"

After a person is born again, the flesh wars against the spirit, and the spirit wars against the flesh. They are continually antagonistic toward each other (see Galatians 5). The Bible does not say the lusts of the flesh will go away and you will never be tempted. The flesh will keep warring against the spirit, screaming demands at you that will lead you into trouble if you continually walk according to the flesh: "Give me a banana split." "Buy those clothes and charge them to a credit card." "I want a donut." "I want a donut again today." "I want two donuts today." "I want three donuts today." "Where are my donuts? Drive to the store and buy my donuts."

The Bible does say if you walk in the spirit, you will not fulfill the lusts of the flesh. To live in victory, a believer must understand the functions of the spirit, the soul, and the body and know how to discern the difference between the leading of the Holy Spirit and the desires of the flesh—what it thinks and feels and wants. A believer must know how to follow the leading of the Holy Spirit, or as the Bible calls it, "walking in the Spirit" (see Galatians 5:25), in order not to fulfill the lusts of the flesh.

Spirit and soul should work together, and the body should act as a servant to both. You walk in the spirit by learning to make right choices, and letting the Holy Spirit who raised Jesus from the dead, Who now lives in your spirit, empower you.

SECTION I

Your Spirit—The Real You

CHAPTER 7

Do You Want Misery, Mediocrity, or Victory?

I am convinced only a few people ever enjoy the fulfillment of God's perfect plan for their lives because they don't know how to listen to God's leading or know how to follow Him. We can live the abundant life if we learn to listen to the leading of the Holy Spirit who came to live in us at our new birth.

Even though I had accepted Jesus as my Savior, sincerely loved and wanted to obey Him, and was very active in church for years, I was miserable. I understood I was saved by faith and would go to heaven, but I did not live in victory and was not affecting anybody else in a positive way. I am not sure my daily witness would have encouraged anyone else to make a commitment to Jesus.

During all those years as a Christian, I didn't realize God wanted to communicate directly with me. I certainly didn't understand He intended for me to enjoy victory in my daily living and simply enjoy life itself. I was unhappy and dissatisfied, and people like that usually make others unhappy. I went to church on Sunday but it was not enough. I longed for a deeper relationship with God and I did not know how to have one. Just going to church and trying to follow rules would never give me the deep contentment and joy for which I longed.

As I sought God for something deeper, He began teaching me His Word and it renewed my mind and changed the way I thought about everything. Through His Word, He helped me understand He does want to communicate with us individually and has a plan for our lives to take us to a place of peace and contentment. God's will is for us to attain knowledge of His plan through His divine guidance. We should do good works, but they should be done out of our relationship with God and not as a method of trying to earn something from Him. I serve Him because I love Him, not to get Him to love me. God's love for us is unconditional. He cannot be bought with good works.

> God does want to communicate with us individually and has a plan for our lives to take us to a place of peace and contentment.

Knowledge is progressive and we don't learn everything we need to know about Jesus overnight. Jesus told His disciples He still had many things to say to them, but they would not be able to grasp everything then. Jesus was going away, but the Father would send the Spirit of Truth to guide them and to teach them all things and bring to their remembrance everything Jesus told them. It was advantageous to them for Him to go away, because without His leaving, the Comforter (Counselor, Helper Advocate, Intercessor, Strengthener, Standby)—the Holy Spirit—would not come to them.

When Jesus spoke these words He was talking to men with whom He had spent the previous three years. They were with Him day and night, yet He indicated He had more to teach them. You would think if Jesus was with you personally for three years, day and night, you could learn all there is to know. From a human perspective, I think if I had one uninterrupted month with people, I could tell them everything I know, but Jesus said to expect more. He was telling the disciples, and us through His words recorded in the Bible, He will always have something to say to us about new situations we are facing. The Father would send His Holy Spirit to them, and us, to help. The Holy Spirit would lead us into all truth, advise us, and empower us to live the life God desires for us.

When we receive Jesus, we become adopted sons and daughters of God. Everything Jesus has is ours in our joint inheritance. We need only learn how to receive it by faith, and that means we may not always feel or see anything, but we choose to believe God's Word as truth. Jesus became flesh and experienced the types of things we experience and understands our needs (see Hebrews 4:15–16). He was led by the Spirit, just as we can be led by the Spirit. He overcame temptation, just as we can overcome temptation. He chose to come to earth in a fleshly body so He could be our High Priest and understand everything we go through.

Jesus was confined to a body, just as we are, and could only be in one place at a time. But the Holy Spirit is able to be in every single one of us everywhere we go, all the time, individually leading and guiding us. God knew we would need help in understanding His plan for us and sent the Holy Spirit to dwell inside every believer. The Holy Spirit tells us what He hears from the Father. The Holy Spirit is our Guide, our Teacher of Truth, our Counselor, our Helper, and our Comforter (see John 16:7). He will never leave us nor forsake us. When we learn how to listen to Him and follow His leading, we can trust Him to lead us on the right path every day.

CHAPTER 8

Follow His Lead

There are three functions of your spirit. The first is fellowshipping with God. The spirit is the place where you fellowship with God and the place you really hear from Him. The second is intuition or discernment. Intuitive living by your spirit comes with learning to "hear" God inside yourself in a way the Bible calls "a still, small voice" (1 Kings 19:12). It is an inward witness, a peace, a spiritual knowing different from head knowledge or intellect. It is a way of knowing things that don't come from stored knowledge or because you learned them somewhere along the line. It is a deeper knowing, a sensing of truth. Life is so much easier when we simply follow the inward witness rather than ignore it. This means if you don't have peace about something, don't do it.

There are times when I know that something is not right for me to do and I don't even know why. Everyone else might be doing it, but I sense in my spirit it is not what God desires for me. I have learned to trust that "inward witness" even more than I trust my own thoughts, feelings, or will. It took a long time to make the transition, but life is much better now that I have.

The third function of the spirit is conscience. Your conscience is the best preacher you'll ever hear, and it preaches to you all day long. Many people have no personal relationship with God, no real fellowship with Him, because they have a seared or hardened conscience. They have ignored their conscience for so long it is no longer soft and tender. They are able to do wrong things and not sense much conviction. Pray that God will soften your conscience and learn to listen to it because it is God trying to speak to you.

There are also people who have an overactive conscience. They tend to feel guilty about everything. The only remedy for this is a thorough study of God's Word in order to learn what God's will really is. He wants us to enjoy a life of freedom, yet not use that freedom as an excuse to sin.

Walking in the Spirit means listening to the advice your friend Jesus is giving you through learning the Word and listening to God's Spirit living in you. It means following your enlightened conscience and not doing something if you don't have peace about it; basically, doing what God tells you to do. If you are not accustomed to walking in the Spirit, it will take time to learn how to do it. But God is patient and will continue to teach and change you.

Walking in the Spirit means listening to the advice your friend Jesus is giving you through learning the Word and listening to God's Spirit living in you.

Over the last few years, I've developed a habit of occasionally stopping for a minute to see what I sense in my spirit about something. When the devil is putting wrong thoughts into your head, accusing you of being incapable or unable to succeed, it is amazing how taking a minute to hear from God will set you back on track.

In the early years of my ministry, my mind would start telling me, *You're not going to make it. This is not going to work—it's stupid. Nobody cares what you're doing. You're not even hearing from God, anyway. You have no business trying to teach people anything.* The enemy, the devil, was using those kinds of thoughts to accuse me and keep me from working for God. You may have times in your life when your thoughts are saying, *Give up* and your feelings are right in line. You want to give up; you feel like giving up, perhaps other people even tell you to give up, then you get quiet somewhere for a minute and say, "Now, Lord, what do You have to say about this?" You will hear Him say, "Keep on pressing forward and never give up." No wonder the Bible says in Psalm 46:10 (KJV), "Be still, and know that I am God."

The closer you grow to God, the easier it is to develop a lifestyle of making the right choices. Philippians 2:12 says to work out your own salvation with fear and trembling. This means after your salvation at the new birth, you build your relationship with God by studying, learning, praying, and fellowshipping with God. You let your relationship with Him affect every area of your life. God is not willing to live in what I call a "Sunday morning box." He wants to invade every day of your life and be involved in everything you do. I encourage you to turn your will over to God and let the Holy Spirit work that salvation through your soul—let Him think through your mind, teach you to love what He loves, and use your emotions and your will to serve Him. Many people would be comfortable using all their emotions at a football game, but they feel uncomfortable displaying emotions in their worship of God. We need to realize that He wants us to use everything He has given us in serving Him. Make all of your resources available to God. Be willing to use your energy, talents, and finances in serving Him. As you let His light shine through you, it affects the people around you in a positive way and they begin to want to know Jesus too.

CHAPTER 9

The Right Truth at the Right Time

When Jesus told His disciples the Father would send the Spirit of Truth to guide them into all truth, He was describing a method the Holy Spirit uses to free us in areas where we struggle. In 1976 I reached a point in my life when the Holy Spirit knew I was ready to face truth and let Him do a thorough work of healing in my life.

Many of us live in a false reality we have developed to protect ourselves. I spent a lot of my life avoiding issues that needed to be dealt with. I blamed other people, felt sorry for myself, and had a bad attitude, but none of that was changing any of my circumstances. One of my difficulties was developing and maintaining good relationships. I was convinced all the other people in my life were the problem, and they were the ones who needed to change for us to get along.

One day, as usual, I was praying for my husband to change in some area, when the Holy Spirit began revealing a truth to me He knew I was ready to face. As He began speaking to my heart—impressing on me the truth I needed to see—I saw the source of the problems I had been blaming on everyone and everything else. As I was praying, the Holy Spirit caused me to realize the source of the problem was not my husband. The source of the problem was me! I was devastated emotionally for three days as I looked in shock at the extent of the deception into which I had led myself by believing everyone except me was the problem. The Holy Spirit gently unveiled the truth to me of what life was like for the members of my family who had to live in the same house with me. I saw I was hard to get along with, impossible to keep happy, critical, selfish, dominating, controlling, manipulative, negative, nagging—and this was just the beginning of the list.

It was extremely difficult for me to face this truth, but as the Holy Spirit gave me the grace to do it, in that year I began a life of learning how to cooperate with the Holy Spirit working inside me to transform the ashes in my life into beauty. My life became a series of new freedoms, each preceded by a new truth the Holy Spirit revealed to me. Many of the truths I teach people today came out of that initial truth the Spirit of Truth led me to in 1976.

Truth is wonderful. Jesus said it will make us free. But as wonderful as truth is, we must be ready to face it. Truth is often harsh; it shocks us into a reality we may feel unprepared to see, but if God is revealing it He knows the time is right. As tough as it might be at the time to press through the pain rather than avoiding it, we will be so glad to live in the freedom and rewards it brings.

Truth is often harsh; it shocks us into a reality we may feel unprepared to see, but if God is revealing it He knows the time is right.

I strongly urge you to be willing to face truth because there is no freedom without it. The world is filled with deception and the Bible actually teaches us that it will get worse as time goes by. God said that if He did not shorten the days for the sake of the very elect, no man could stand the deception coming to the earth. It is very common today for someone to call evil good and good evil. We must not look to the world to teach us how to live sincere, truthful lives, but rather to the Word of God and the Holy Spirit.

> Let our lives lovingly express truth [in all things, speaking truly, dealing truly, living truly]. Enfolded in love, let us grow up in every way *and* in all things into Him Who is the Head, [even] Christ (the Messiah, the Anointed One) (Ephesians 4:15).

CHAPTER 10

Learn to Hear from God

Learning to hear from God and being led by the Holy Spirit is very exciting. God wants to speak to us about the plan He has for our lives. His plan is a good plan, but we are in danger of missing it if we don't learn how to listen to and obey God's voice.

We talk to our children all the time—why wouldn't our heavenly Father talk to His children? We would not expect our children to know what we wanted them to do if we did not talk to them, so why would God feel any different?

> We would not expect our children to know what we wanted them to do if we did not talk to them, so why would God feel any different?

God speaks to us in many ways. He speaks to us through His Holy Spirit dwelling in us, through that "knowing" deep inside us, and through peace. He may also speak through nature, other people, circumstances, wisdom, supernatural intervention, dreams, and visions.

God also speaks through our conscience, our desires, and an audible voice. However, the two most prevalent ways God speaks to us are through His Word and the inward witness in our hearts. Hearing the audible voice of God is rare for most people and nonexistent for many. I have heard the audible voice of God three or four times in my life. Two of those times were at night when I was awakened by His voice simply calling my name. All I heard was, "Joyce," but I knew it was God calling me. He did not say what He wanted, but I knew instinctively it had something to do with a ministry call on my life, although clarity did not come in that area for several more years.

I heard the audible voice of God in February 1976, a very significant year for me, the day I was filled with the Holy Spirit. That morning, I cried out to God about how awful life was, and I told Him something was missing in my relationship with Him. I felt I was at the end of my rope.

His voice seemed to fill my entire car, and He simply said, "Joyce, I have been teaching you patience." Since that was my first time to hear anything of that magnitude, it both thrilled and shocked me. I instinctively knew what He meant. I had asked God several months prior to that time to teach me patience, not realizing the lesson would include a lengthy period of feeling my life was on hold. The frustration of that feeling peaked that morning in February when I cried out to God in desperation asking Him to do something and give me whatever it was I was missing.

When I heard God's voice, I was suddenly filled with faith that He was going to do something wonderful in my life, although I did not know what it would be; I spent the day in expectation and thanksgiving. That evening in my car, while returning home from my job, God's Spirit touched me in a special way and filled me with His Presence. This event was the beginning of a new level in my relationship with God.

Ask God to help you learn how to listen to Him, to be sensitive to His voice. He wants to talk to you, to develop a closer relationship with you. It is your privilege and right as a born-again believer in Jesus Christ to fellowship daily with God the Father, Jesus Christ His Son, and the Holy Spirit. Learn to talk to God about absolutely everything. God is interested in everything that concerns you.

CHAPTER 11

The Life of God Is Inside Us

The Holy Spirit acts somewhat like a traffic policeman inside me. When I do the right things, I get a "green light" from Him, and when I do wrong things, I get a "red light." If I am about to get myself in trouble, but I have not fully made a decision to proceed, I get a "caution signal."

The more we stop and ask God for directions, the more sensitive we become to the signals within from the Holy Spirit. He doesn't scream and yell at us; He simply whispers in the still, small voice and lets us know we are about to make a mistake. Each time we listen and obey, it becomes easier to hear Him the next time. He will always lead us to newness of life and inner peace, if we yield to Him.

As believers, we have the life of God inside us. *We are the dwelling place or home of God.* I believe this truth is necessary for each of us to understand in order to enjoy close fellowship and intimacy with God.

Why would God want to live in us? And how can He? After all, He is holy, and we are weak humans with frailties, faults, and failures. We are to simply believe that Jesus' sacrifice for our sins was enough to allow us into the presence of God. God takes up residence within us when we give our lives to Jesus by believing in Him as the only Savior and Lord. From that position He, by the power of the Holy Spirit, begins a wonderful work in us. This truth is so awesome that it is difficult for our finite minds to grasp and believe.

The answer is this: He loves us and chooses to make His home in us. He does that because He is God—He has the ability to do what He wants, and He chooses to make His home in our hearts. This choice is based not on any good deeds we have done or ever could do, but solely on the grace (or power), mercy, and love of God. As believers in Christ, we become God's dwelling place (see Ephesians 3:17; 2 Timothy 1:14; 1 John 4:15).

Also difficult for our finite minds to grasp and believe is that God wants to be involved in even the smallest details of our lives. Don't ever hesitate to take what you think are small things to God. After all, *everything* is small to God. Sometimes we act as if we will tax God's ability if we ask Him for too much help. I remember a woman who came to me for prayer and wanted to know if it would be all right if she asked God for two things. If not, she assured me that she would only ask for one. It always makes me sad when I hear people say things like that. I want everyone to know how generous God is and that He wants to give even more than we know how to ask for. You have not because you ask not (see James 4:2), so go ahead and ask boldly because it is God's will that you do so.

> God wants to be involved in even the smallest details of our lives.

It is vital to know what God's Word says about His role in your life, because it confirms His divine plan to be intimately involved with all that concerns you. God's Word says to acknowledge Him in *all our ways* and He will direct our paths (see Proverbs 3:6). To acknowledge God simply means to care what He thinks and to ask for His opinion. Proverbs 3:7 says, "Be not wise in your own eyes." In other words, don't even think you can run your life and do a good job without God's help and direction. It takes most of us far too long to learn this important lesson.

The world makes it easy for us to fill our ears with all kinds of things that drown out the voice of God and place Him far in the background of our lives. However, the day comes for every person when only God remains. Everything else in life is currently passing away; and when it does, God will still be here.

Nothing can satisfy our longing for God, except communion and fellowship with Him. Hearing from God is vital to enjoying God's eternal plan for our lives. Listening to God is our decision; no one else can make it for us. God won't *force* us to choose His will, but He will do everything He can to *encourage* us to say yes to His ways.

CHAPTER 12

The Most Direct Way

An experience my husband and I had reminded me of the way life goes when we think living the way we want is better than following the leading of God's Holy Spirit. When Dave and I travel, we sometimes hire a guide to show us the best and most important places to see. One time we decided to explore without following a guide. We thought we would have a better experience by doing what we wanted, when we wanted. Instead, we quickly discovered our independent trips were almost a complete waste of time. We spent a large part of the day losing our way and another large part of the day trying to find the way out. The experience of wandering aimlessly trying to find particular places taught us following a guide is a much wiser use of our time.

The Holy Spirit is ready to guide us all day, every day. When we go our own way, thinking a life of doing what we want to do when we want to do it will be good, we lose so much time trying to find our way, we can waste our entire lives. God is committed to guiding us. Learning how to hear and follow Him is very important.

The Bible is full of great promises for our individual walk with God. The Lord will lead us step by step. By faith, we take the step He has shown us, and then He gives us the next one. At times we may stumble and fall down, but He always helps us back up. We continue forward in His strength and His grace, knowing that every time we face a fork in the road God will guide us.

God wants us to care about what He thinks, and quite often if we show we do by seeking Him, He responds by saying, "Do all that is in your heart, I am with you in all that you do." God is not a dictator; He is our Divine Partner in life. He allows us the freedom of making many choices. When we receive Jesus as Savior, God gives us a new heart and puts His Spirit in us (see Ezekiel 36:26). He writes His law (His will) in our hearts and expects us to follow what we find there. It is important that we do not over-spiritualize hearing from God and make it a difficult thing to do. The longer you walk with God, the easier it is to follow Him.

God is not a dictator; He is our Divine Partner in life. He allows us the freedom of making many choices.

God will guide us in the way to go, but then we have to do the walking. A walk with God takes place through one step of obedience at a time. Some people want the entire blueprint for their lives before making one decision. God does not usually operate that way. He leads us one step at a time.

CHAPTER 13

Looking Ahead

One of the many benefits of hearing from God is the help He gives us to prepare for the future. The Holy Spirit gives us the message the Father gave Him. He declares to us things that will happen in the future.

We see many instances in the Bible when God gave people information about the future. Noah was told to prepare for a flood (see Genesis 6:13–17). When Moses was told to go to Pharaoh and ask for the release of the Israelites, he was also told Pharaoh would not let them go (see Exodus 7). Obviously, God does not tell us everything that will happen in the future, but the Bible says He will tell us of things to come.

There are times when I can sense inside my spirit that something good is going to happen, or at times something challenging. Of course when I sense something challenging is about to happen, I always hope I am wrong and that it is just my imagination, but if I am right, then having the knowledge ahead of time acts as a shock absorber in my life. If an automobile has good shock absorbers on it and hits a hole in the road, it cushions the impact for the passengers and no one gets hurt. God giving us information ahead of time serves the same purpose.

I remember many times like this, but one in particular was when I felt strongly inside my heart that one of my children was really struggling with something major. When I asked, my child told me everything was just fine, but by the Spirit I knew something was wrong. Several days later I received some news that was painful and discouraging, but it would have been a lot more difficult had I not been given a previous warning.

First Corinthians 2:5 teaches us to put our faith not in the wisdom of men (human philosophy) but in the power of God. Verse 11 says no one discerns the thoughts of God except the Spirit of God. Since the Holy Spirit knows the secret counsels of God, it is vital for us to know how to hear what He wants to say to us. The Holy Spirit will help us realize and comprehend and appreciate the gifts of divine favor and blessings God bestows on us. Human wisdom doesn't teach us this truth, but it is from the Holy Spirit who gives us the mind of Christ (see vv. 12–13).

The Holy Spirit knows both the mind of God and God's individual plan for you. His road map for you is not necessarily like anybody else's, so it doesn't work to try to pattern your life after what someone else heard from God. God has a unique plan for you, and the Holy Spirit knows what it is and will reveal it to you. You must get comfortable being an individual who is not like everyone else. God likes creativity and He moves in a variety of ways.

When God shows us something that is to take place in the future, He rarely tells us the exact time it will take place. This can be frustrating to us unless we learn to trust God's timing. The Bible says our times are in His hands. God put a dream in my heart to teach His Word to large numbers of people. I felt very sure I heard from God and began teaching a small Bible study. I spent a lot of time being frustrated because I thought everything would happen right away. I did not know that God's way is usually to start small and gradually allow growth as we prove we are capable of handling it. I encourage you to enjoy where you are at on the way to where you are going. Enjoy today while you embrace tomorrow by faith. Do not despise the day of small beginnings and always remember God may not show up early, but He will *never* be late.

> Enjoy where you are at on the way to where you are going.

CHAPTER 14

Do You Have Selective Hearing?

Recently God told me that when we are *unwilling* to hear in one area, it may render us *unable* to hear in other areas. Sometimes we choose to turn a deaf ear to what we know the Lord is clearly saying to us. We only hear what we want to hear, which is called "selective hearing." After a while, people think they can't hear from God anymore but really, there are many things they already know He wants them to respond to, but they haven't done so. I have learned that the more quickly I do whatever it is the Lord tells me to do, the more quickly He reveals the next step I am to take.

A woman once shared with me that she asked God to give her direction concerning what He wanted her to do. He clearly put in her heart that He wanted her to forgive her sister for an offense that happened between them months before. Because she wasn't willing to forgive, she pulled away from her prayer time. When she did seek the Lord again for something, He always responded, "Forgive your sister first."

Over a period of *two years*, every time she asked the Lord for guidance in something new, He gently reminded her, "I want you to forgive your sister." Finally, she realized she would never grow spiritually if she didn't do the last thing God told her to do.

She got on her knees and prayed, "Lord, give me the power to forgive my sister." Instantly she understood many things from her sibling's perspective she hadn't considered before and within a short time their relationship was healed and stronger than ever before.

If we really want to hear from God, we can't approach Him with selective hearing hoping to narrow the topics to only what we want to hear. People take time to listen for His voice when they have issues *they* want solved. If they have a problem, or have concerns about their job, or need wisdom on how to have more prosperity, or need to deal with a child, they are all ears to hear what God has to say.

Don't just go to God and talk to Him when you want or need something; also spend time with Him—just listening. He will open up many issues if you will be still before Him and simply listen. As we study God's Word, we are confronted with many things that will need to change in our lives in order for us to be what God desires us to be. If we are willing, God will do the work; but if we make excuses and have selective hearing, we will remain in bondage and darkness and hearing from God will become more and more difficult.

For many people, listening is an ability only developed by practice. I have always been a talker; I never had to try to talk. But I have had to learn to listen on purpose. The Bible says, "Be still, and know that I am God" (Psalm 46:10 NIV). Our flesh is full of energy and usually wants to be active doing something, so it can be difficult to be still.

As I said, talking has always been easy for me. I told my husband one day we needed to talk more. It seemed to me he never wanted to spend time just sitting and talking. He responded by saying, "Joyce, *we* don't talk, you talk and I listen." He was right and I needed to change if I expected him to want to fellowship with me. I also discovered I was doing the same thing with God; I talked and expected God to listen. I complained that I never heard from God, but the truth was I never listened.

When you ask God a question, take some time and listen. Even if He does not respond right at that moment, He will in due time. You may be doing some ordinary task when God decides to speak, but if you have honored Him by listening as part of your fellowship with Him, He will speak at the right time.

> You may be doing some ordinary task when God decides to speak, but if you have honored Him by listening as part of your fellowship with Him, He will speak at the right time.

Please don't fall into a trap of listening for voices. Remember that God speaks in a variety of ways, and His most usual ways are through His Word and the inward witness which often manifests as a strong "knowing." He may also work through circumstances or some other very normal things. I wrote a book titled *How to Hear from God*, and I suggest it for anyone who really wants to learn more about this important subject.

CHAPTER 15

Let the Holy Spirit Defend You

Most of us spend a great deal of time and energy in life trying to defend ourselves, our reputation, our position, our actions, our words, and our decisions. We are truly wasting a great deal of our time. When people are judgmental in nature or character and are judgmental toward us, we may finally after much effort convince them of our purity of heart. But with a judgmental nature, they will quickly find something else about us to judge. In these types of situations, it is best to pray and let God be our defense.

This gives us much to think about. The Holy Spirit as Comforter to us is called to our side to give us aid in every way. When we need defense, He acts as a legal assistant would for a client, a counsel for our defense to plead our case, an intercessor for us. It is good to know we don't have to defend ourselves when we are accused of something; we can ask for help from the Holy One and expect to receive it. He is our Advocate. Just thinking about that should bring us comfort.

> We don't have to defend ourselves when we are accused of something; we can ask for help from the Holy One and expect to receive it.

We notice in the Holy Scriptures that Jesus basically never defended Himself. Philippians 2:7 (KJV) says He "made himself of no reputation." He didn't try to make one, and therefore He did not have to worry about keeping it.

After years of trying to be well thought of, I discovered that it is much better to have a good reputation in heaven than on earth. I want to have a good reputation with people, and hopefully, I live my life in such a way that I do. But I don't worry about it anymore. I do my best and let God take care of the rest.

Romans 8:33 tells us it is God who justifies us; we don't have to justify ourselves, not even to God the Father. Why should we then have to try to justify ourselves before people? We don't have to when we understand the Holy Spirit is our Advocate.

Not needing to defend ourselves, but instead trusting God to be our Vindicator, is just one of many privileges and freedoms that are ours as we enter into a new life lived with Jesus as our Savior. Once we receive Him we begin an exciting journey. Sometimes the journey is difficult, but our most difficult day with Jesus will be far better than our best day ever was without Him. Make a decision to enjoy your journey. As you walk with God you will learn, and as you apply what you learn you will experience more and more freedom and joy.

Some of the things that are yours in Christ are peace, righteousness, joy, strength, hope, love, power, wisdom, prudence (good management), provision to meet your needs, heaven, and many other things too numerous to mention. Expect great things in life because we serve a great God! Listen and obey each step of the way and you will surely enjoy a life worth living.

CHAPTER 16

Listen for God's Still, Small Voice

Someone once told me of a one-act play with three characters—a father, a mother, and a son who had just returned from Viet Nam—sitting at a table talking. The play lasts thirty minutes, and they all get their chance to talk. There's only one problem: no one listens to the others.

The father is about to lose his job. The mother who once held just about every office in their church is now being pushed aside by younger women. The son struggles with his faith. He had gone to war, saw chaos and death, and is now bewildered about life.

At the end of the play, the son stands and heads toward the door. "You haven't heard a word I've said" is his parting remark, as he walks out of the room. The parents look at each other, and the mother asks, "What did he mean?"

What the parents didn't get—and the audience obviously did—is that the son struggled to believe in a loving, caring God. Every time he tried to explain, one of the parents interrupted with something the parent wanted to say. The soldier needed to hear from God. Hoping his mother or father would be the channel through which God would speak, he went to them. However, they were not available for God's use because they were not quiet enough to hear Him. All three of them were so distraught and noisy; they all left the same way they came. What might have happened had they really listened to one another then quietly prayed and waited on God? I am sure the outcome would have been very different and much more rewarding.

In 1 Kings 19, we read of the deeply committed prophet Elijah, who defied the wicked King Ahab and Queen Jezebel for years. The big moment came on Mount Carmel when Elijah destroyed 450 prophets of Baal. Later, when Queen Jezebel threatened to kill him, he ran away, apparently in terror.

Elijah went into a cave to hide out. He must have been worn out by the powerful events. Suddenly the man was alone, with no crowds, no one trying to kill him, and no one to talk to. When God asked him what he was doing there, Elijah spoke of his zeal for Him. Then he told God the children of Israel had gone astray, killing prophets, "And I, I only, am left; and they seek my life, to take it away" (v. 10). God told Elijah, "Go out and stand on the mount before the Lord" (v. 11).

God brought strong winds, falling rocks, an earthquake, and fire. I think that was the way Elijah expected God to appear—in the miraculous and powerful. But the writer tells us God wasn't in those things. "And behold, the Lord passed by, and a great and strong wind rent the mountains and broke in pieces the rocks before the Lord, but the Lord was not in the wind; and after the wind an earthquake, but the Lord was not in the earthquake; and after the earthquake a fire, but the Lord was not in the fire; and after the fire [a sound of gentle stillness and] a still, small voice (vv. 11–12).

As long as Elijah sought the dramatic, he didn't hear God. But when he pulled back and listened for the inner voice, the soft, non-demanding voice of the Holy Spirit, Elijah could communicate with God.

> Do you take time to be quiet and just listen?

What kind of voice are you expecting to hear from God? Will you recognize the still, small voice when you hear it? Do you take time to be quiet and just listen? Ask Him to help you listen most of all in the soft stillness for the quiet ways in which He speaks.

CHAPTER 17

My New Start

On a Friday morning in February 1976, I was driving to work and feeling discouraged. My husband and I had an argument before I left for work—something that happened quite often. I was quite disheartened because little in my life seemed to be working. Although I was making every effort to be what I thought was a good Christian by attending church and following their rules, none of it seemed to be working. I was not experiencing the peace and joy promised in the Scriptures.

Dave was an elder at our church, and I was the first and only woman at that time to serve on the church board. Helping make decisions in the church was extremely frustrating because of all the bureaucracy. Often it took several meetings just to decide a small, almost insignificant matter. The church was filled with people vying for positions, and I saw very little real love.

Dave and I were both on the Evangelism Team, who one night a week went door-to-door telling others about Jesus. Our life revolved around the church. Our children went to school there. We joined all the right social clubs and sports teams and attended all the church dinners. We thought we had good friends, but I was soon to discover otherwise.

I felt I needed change in my life, but I didn't know exactly what I needed. I was searching, but I didn't know what I was searching for. Out of sheer frustration and desperation that morning in the car, I cried out to God. I told Him I felt I couldn't go on any longer with the way things were. I remember saying, "God, something is missing. I don't know what it is, but something is missing."

I was so spiritually hungry I was ready to receive anything as long as I knew it was from God. I was like a starving person. People can be hungry but still picky about what they eat; however, if they get hungry enough, they will eat whatever is put before them. Because of my great spiritual hunger, I was totally open to God at that point in my life.

To my surprise I heard the audible voice of God that morning in my car. He called my name and spoke to me about patience. From that moment, my heart filled with faith and I knew with certainty God was going to do something about my situation. I didn't know what He would do or when, but I knew He was about to move in my life.

On Fridays after work, I had my hair done. Friday evenings, Dave and I always went bowling as part of a league. On that Friday late afternoon, I drove home from the beauty shop, turning off Highway 270 onto the Gravois exit to go to Fenton, the St. Louis suburb where we lived. As I sat in the car at a red light, I felt my heart fill with faith about what God was going to do. Even though I had no idea what it would be, I began to thank Him for it.

At that very moment, Jesus filled me with the presence of the Holy Spirit in a way that I had never before experienced. I didn't know what was taking place, but I certainly knew God manifested Himself in a different and powerful way. The best way I can describe my feeling at that moment is to say it was as if someone poured me full of liquid love. The experience affected my behavior. I was peaceful, happy, excited, and easy to get along with. I felt as if I loved everything and everyone.

I remember driving past a field of weeds and thinking how beautiful they were, simply because I knew God made them. Everything God had anything to do with looked beautiful to me. People I hadn't wanted to be around before suddenly seemed pleasant and likeable to me. I was actually the one who was different, but when we change, everyone and everything else seems to us to have changed. After that experience with God, my behavior changed to the extent that people began asking me what happened. All I knew to tell them was that God was wonderful. My new enthusiasm seemed to start rubbing off on others, and before long I was teaching a Bible study at work.

If you are not satisfied with your relationship with God, there is always more to know about Him. We are to seek the Lord, not an experience, and He alone decides how and when to manifest His presence in our lives. He deals with each of us individually, but He does promise that if we seek Him, we will find Him. If we ask the Father to give us the Holy Spirit in a greater measure, He will do it.

> We are to seek the Lord, not an experience, and He alone decides how and when to manifest His presence in our lives.

I started that day feeling as if everything had come to a discouraging end. But that night, I went to bed knowing I was at a place of new beginnings. That is how God is. He often moves suddenly in our lives. God is faithful and ever true to His word (see Hebrews 10:23). He is no respecter of persons—what is available to one is available to all. God may not answer each of us exactly the same way, but He will answer our prayers and meet our needs.

Our seeking must be sincere and we should always be ready to make a deeper commitment. When that is the case, God will move and send His Holy Spirit to touch each of us in a special way. Ask and believe by faith that God will do something wonderful. While you wait for Him to do it, thank Him, and offer Him praise. Open yourself up to Him and tell Him you want everything He has for you.

What are you pursuing in life? Is it money, position or popularity? I encourage you to make the pursuit of God your number one goal in life. If you seek Him with your whole heart you will find Him. If you seek Him sincerely He will reveal Himself to you. One touch or one word from God can change your life forever.

CHAPTER 18

Spiritual Weapons

The weapons of our warfare are not of the natural realm. Second Corinthians 10:4 tells us, "The weapons of our warfare are not carnal but mighty in God for pulling down strongholds" (KJV). Our weapons are spiritual because our battle is not with flesh and blood.

We have the power of God's Word, the authority of Jesus through the use of His name, and the blood He shed for our forgiveness of sin, healing, and protection.

What's in a name? A lot more than most of us realize. When we call a person by name we are making a declaration about that individual. By calling Sarai "Sarah," Abraham and all of those who spoke her name were helping to change her image of herself.

Sarai was a barren woman, a woman who probably had a poor self-image because she had not been able to give her husband a child. She was an old woman, and in conventional thinking had no hope of her situation ever being any different, but God changed her name! Everyone who called her Sarah was calling her a princess. She must have begun to see herself differently. She must have felt faith rising in her heart. By calling her Sarah, or Princess, like God they were literally "call[ing] those things which be not as though they were" (Romans 4:17 KJV).

The same is true when we speak the name of Jesus. It is not just a name, but a declaration of His character and, what He has come to do; it declares all He has accomplished. As the Gospel of John states, "whatever you ask the Father in My Name [as presenting all that I AM]" (John 15:16 AMP). Even His name carries immeasurable power. His name represents Him.

When God appeared to Moses in a burning bush, Moses asked who he should say sent him. God responded with, "I Am." It should be enough for us to know the Lord is with us and He is everything we need now—or ever will need.

Jesus' name is above every other name there is. He has given us the authority to represent everything He is in His name (see Ephesians 1:21; Philippians 2:9). Jesus' name is above all names, and by using the authority of His name we have power over the works of the devil. Jesus came to earth so we could have life more abundantly. He defeated the devil's power with the blood He shed.

> Jesus' name is above every other name there is. He has given us the authority to represent everything He is in His name.

Ephesians 6 tells of the spiritual weapons of defense which include the breastplate of righteousness, the belt of truth, the shoes of peace, the shield of faith, the helmet of salvation, and one offensive weapon—the sword the Spirit wields, which is the Word of God.

And God's Word is more powerful than a two-edged sword, so powerful it can divide soul and spirit. A sword is a weapon with which one attacks an enemy. A sword in the sheath is of no value. It must be wielded, or taken from the sheath and appropriately used. The Word of God is the believer's sword, and he must learn to apply it accurately.

The Holy Spirit will often protect an individual against attack even before the attack becomes evident to him if he has learned to wield the sword of the Spirit. As he does so, the Holy Spirit applies the right scripture to the problem. For example, if a person feels grouchy and impatient, scriptures on financial success won't help him. But scriptures on kindness, love, and not being moved by feelings will strengthen him and help him walk in victory above his feelings. We can see why learning the Word of God is so important.

In my own life I find that when I am faced with problems or challenges, scriptures or Scripture-based songs will *rise within me.*

I have learned to speak them out, sing them, or meditate on them even when I do not particularly know what may be transpiring in the spiritual realm. I believe the way the Spirit wields the sword is by the Holy Spirit in the believer knowing exactly what scripture to use in every situation. He knows precisely what type of attack the believer is encountering.

The Word is alive and powerful. When we speak God's Word, it contains the power to accomplish what it says it will do.

The Word of God holds power for the believer who has understanding concerning the blood of Jesus. Under the Old Covenant, the high priest offered atonement for the people's sins once a year. Under the New Covenant, Jesus became the only sacrifice needed for sin. Through shedding His blood on the cross, dying for our sins, and rising from the dead, He gave new life to those who believe in Him. He restored mankind's relationship with God—the relationship lost in the Garden of Eden when mankind disobeyed God, separating us from Him.

The New Covenant shows us a new way of living. We can live by faith in Jesus and actually enjoy everything He purchased with His death and resurrection.

Jesus died to give us a new life, but the devil will try to deceive us and steal that life unless we have instruction on how to use our powerful weapons of warfare to defeat him.

Jesus has promised to be with us always (see Matthew 28:20). We can win every battle we face in life because we have the power of God on our side.

SECTION II

Your Soul—Mind, Will, and Emotions

Your Mind

CHAPTER 19

A New Way of Thinking

When God begins to deal with us about wrong behavior, it's easy enough to say, "I can't help it," but it takes real courage and faith to say, "I'm ready to take responsibility and get my life straightened out." Avoidance, or not facing issues, is a major problem. Wrong things don't go away just because we refuse to acknowledge them. We often stuff things. We hide from them, and as long as we do, they have power over us.

For many years, I refused to deal with the sexual abuse in my childhood. My father abused me, so I left home the week I turned eighteen. I thought I was getting away from the problem by leaving, but I didn't realize the problem had infested my soul. It was in my thoughts, attitudes, and words. It affected my actions and all my relationships. I buried my past and stuffed my stuff. We don't have to live in the past—in fact, we are encouraged by God's Word to forget it and let it go. However, that doesn't mean we are free to ignore the results of it and pretend we are not hurting when we are.

I had a lot of bad behavior and negative attitudes. I also had lots of excuses. I wasn't dealing with anything from the past; I was merely feeling sorry for myself and saying, "I can't help it. It's not my fault I was abused." And it wasn't my fault. But it was my responsibility to let God help me overcome all the bondage I was experiencing as a result of that abuse.

God began setting me free by dealing with me about all the wrong thoughts I accepted and allowed. Before my life could change, my mind had to change. At first, I didn't even want to take responsibility for my thoughts. I thought, I can't help what I think—things just come into my head! I eventually learned I could choose my own thoughts, and I could think things on purpose. I learned we don't have to accept every thought that falls into our minds. We can cast down wrong ones and replace them with right ones. I learned that instead of feeling helpless over the thoughts filling my mind, I can—I must—do something positive.

We don't have to accept every thought that falls into our minds. We can cast down wrong ones and replace them with right ones.

Much of our thinking is habitual. If we regularly think about God and good things, godly thoughts become natural. Thousands of thoughts flow through our minds every day. We may feel we have no control, but we do. Although we don't have to use any effort to think wrong thoughts, we have to use much effort to think good thoughts. As we begin to make changes, we will have to fight a battle.

The mind is the battlefield, and Satan's primary way of initiating his evil plan for us is through our thoughts. If we feel we have no power over our thoughts, Satan will entrap and defeat us. Instead, we can determine to think in godly ways. We constantly make choices. Where do those choices come from? They originate in our thought life. Our thoughts become our words and our actions.

God has given us the power to decide—to choose right thinking over wrong. But once we make that choice, we must continue to choose right thoughts. It's not a once-and-for-all decision, but it does get easier. The more we fill our lives with reading the Bible, prayer, praise, and fellowship with other believers, the easier it is to continue choosing right thoughts.

It may sound as if I'm saying that trying to live the Christian life is nothing but one continuous struggle. At times we may all feel as if that's true, but that's only a piece of the story. Too many people want to live victorious Christian lives, but they don't want to fight the battles. Victory, however, means winning and overcoming obstacles. We must also remember that living a life of disobedience to God is harder than choosing to live in victory. Yes, there are struggles but they are worth it in the end.

To think in the right way takes practice, and it is not always easy, nor does it feel natural for us to focus only on the good. But if we know this is the pathway to life—both now and in eternity—it's worth the effort and the struggle to think positive thoughts.

When we're bombarded with doubts and fears, that's when we need to take our stand. We don't ever want to say again, "I can't help it." We want to believe and say, "God is with me, and He strengthens me. God enables me to win." The apostle Paul said it this way: "But thanks be to God, Who gives us the victory [making us conquerors] through our Lord Jesus Christ. Therefore, my beloved brethren, be firm (steadfast), immovable, always abounding in the work of the Lord [always being superior, excelling, doing more than enough in the service of the Lord], knowing and being continually aware that your labor in the Lord is not futile [it is never wasted or to no purpose]" (1 Corinthians 15:57–58).

We can choose. Not only can we choose, but we do choose. By not pushing the bad thoughts from our minds, we're allowing them to invade us and take us captive. It takes time to learn to choose good and push away evil. It won't be easy, but we're moving in the right direction every time we take responsibility and make right choices.

CHAPTER 20

Be Careful What You Think

In the early days of computers, they used to say, "Garbage in, garbage out." That was a way of explaining that the computer only worked with the data put into the machine. If we wanted different results, we needed to put in different information.

With computers, most people have no trouble grasping that concept, but when it comes to their minds, they don't seem to get it. Or perhaps they don't want to get it. So many things demand our attention and beg for our focus. And not just sinful things. The apostle Paul said that although everything was lawful for him, not everything was helpful (see 1 Corinthians 6:12).

If you are going to win the battle of the mind and defeat your enemy, where you focus your attention is crucial. The more you meditate on God's Word, the stronger you'll become and the more easily you'll win the victories.

> Those who meditate on God's Word are those who think—and think seriously—about what they're reading.

Too many Christians fail to realize the difference between meditating on the Bible and reading the Bible. They like to think whenever they read God's Word, they're absorbing the deep things of God. Too often people will read a chapter of the Bible, and when they get to the last verse, they have little idea about what they've read. Those who meditate on God's Word are those who think—and think seriously—about what they're reading. They may not put it in these words, but they are saying, "God, speak to me. Teach me. As I ponder Your Word, reveal its depth to me."

Psalm 1 begins by defining the person who is blessed, then points out the right actions of that person. The psalmist wrote that those who meditate—and do it day and night—are like productive trees, and everything they do prospers.

The psalmist made it quite clear that meditating on and thinking about God's Word brings results. As you ponder who God is and what He is saying to you, you will grow. It's really that simple. Another way to put it is to say you become whatever you focus on. If you read about and allow your mind to focus on God's love and power, His love and power operate in you.

The apostle Paul says it beautifully in Philippians 4:8:

> Whatever is true, whatever is worthy of reverence and is honorable and seemly, whatever is just, whatever is pure, whatever is lovely and lovable, whatever is kind and winsome and gracious, if there is any virtue and excellence, if there is anything worthy of praise, think on and weigh and take account of these things [fix your minds on them].

Sadly, most Christians don't put much effort into their study of the Word. They go to hear others teach and preach, and they may listen to sermon tapes and read the Bible occasionally, but they're not dedicated to making God's Word a major part of their lives.

Be careful what you think about. The more you think about good things, the better your life will seem. The more you think about Jesus Christ and the principles He taught, the more you become like Jesus and the stronger you grow. And as you grow, you win the battle for your mind.

One of the things I like to think about is what I can do for other people. Galatians 6:10 says to be mindful to be a blessing to others. To me, that means to have my mind full of ways I can bless other people. I once spent a lot of time thinking about what others could and should do for me, and it only made me unhappy. Now that I've formed a new habit, I find my joy has also increased.

There are many ways to bless people. We can encourage them, compliment them, or help them with a physical need like moving, baby-sitting, or transportation. We can help meet a financial need, we can pray for them, or we can simply listen. Actually, when we help someone, we do more for ourselves than for them. The Bible says it is more blessed to give than to receive. Giving does not always come naturally. The natural man is quite selfish, but learning how to change our thinking can form new habits. Instead of thinking, *What about me?*, think, *It's all about God and other people.*

CHAPTER 21

Meditation Produces Success

When we refer to meditating, we mean to ponder something and give it our full attention. A French couple helped me see that meditation is like eating. They take a bite of food after they have enjoyed the way it looks on the plate. They comment on the pleasant aroma and often mention one or two special ingredients. They chew slowly and deliberately, and they sometimes even comment on how it makes the insides of their mouths feel.

That seems a bit too much for most Americans, but that's a good picture of meditating on God's Word. We don't just wolf down a few words or a verse and hurry on to the next. We pause to reflect on a word, a phrase, or a concept. We compare that scripture with others that come to mind. We feel in no hurry to dash to the end of the chapter. The words are there for us to savor and enjoy. We should learn to be more concerned about quality than quantity. It is more important to grasp a deep understanding of one verse of scripture than it is to read five chapters and understand nothing.

Meditating on God's Word demands discipline. We live in such a fast-paced world few of us make time to meditate. We should form a habit of setting aside time just to sit and think about God's Word and the wonderful promises He made to those who believe in Him. The blessed person mentioned in Psalm 1 is the person who meditates on God's Word "by day and by night" (v. 2). The expression "by day and by night" means it is a major part of a person's life. It's a way of saying that thinking about the Word of God should be a regular part of daily activity. This will require casting down wrong thoughts when they come and choosing to think on things that will benefit us. Keeping ourselves focused will pay off spiritually.

I spend time with God in prayer and in study of His Word each morning, but I also apply the Word to situations I deal with throughout the day. During the writing of this segment, I received some bad news by phone, and my response was to quote and think about various promises in God's Word. His Word strengthens us and helps us keep our peace and joy. For many years all I did when I got bad news was get angry and frustrated and begin to think all negative thoughts. The change in me didn't come because I wished it; I had to choose it, and you will have to do the same thing. It wasn't always easy, but I am sure glad now that I did it.

I titled this chapter "Meditation Produces Success" because it is important for us to understand that contemplating the meaning of scripture isn't simply a good thing to do or an activity reserved for scholars. It is God's command to all of us and a requirement for true success.

> Contemplating the meaning of scripture is God's command to all of us and a requirement for true success.

I thought of the instructions to Joshua as he prepared to lead the people into the Promised Land. The first few verses of the book of Joshua provide God's direction for him. There were at least two million people going into the land, and the responsibility of leading them was immense.

God promised to be with Joshua as He was with Moses, and He urged the new leader to be very courageous. Then He said,

> This Book of the Law shall not depart out of your mouth, but you shall meditate on it day and night, that you may observe and do according to all that is written in it. For then you shall make your way prosperous, and then you shall deal wisely and have good success (Joshua 1:8).

The instructions seem clear. Joshua had the commands of God, and his primary responsibility was to contemplate those words. By immersing himself in the law, he was learning to understand the mind of God more fully. God went on to say that if Joshua kept his mind and heart on the law, he would be prosperous and successful.

Too often people focus on their problems instead of meditating on God's promises. As they do, their problems seem to get bigger, and God's power diminishes. Do you have a problem right now? If so, this is a great time to start practicing your new way of thinking. Think about a breakthrough, not a breakdown. Don't think about the way things are; think about the way they can be with God on your side.

God doesn't want Satan to fill your mind. He doesn't want you to give Satan the opportunity to inject wrong and negative thoughts into your head. For the devil to control your life, all he needs to do is to control your thoughts. Make a decision right now that you will not allow him to do that. Don't let him defeat you. Proverbs 4:20–22 is another scripture that tells of the importance of meditation: "My son, give attention to my words; incline your ear to my sayings. Do not let them depart from your eyes; keep them in the midst of your heart; for they are life to those who find them, and health to all their flesh" (NKJV).

CHAPTER 22

"I Want a Mind Change"

I find a great deal of comfort in thinking about who I used to be and who I have become. It helps me to not be discouraged when I make mistakes or find I still struggle over some issues. I'm greatly encouraged when I consider where I started and where I am now.

In Ephesians 2, Paul describes those outside Christ in verses 1 and 2 as dead (slain) by their trespasses and sins in which they habitually walk and writes that unbelievers follow the prince of the power of the air, who is Satan, and they follow the way their master leads. He also pointed out that all were once dead through their sins, but believers are now alive in Jesus Christ and are not governed nor led by our lower nature—the impulses of our lusts and ungodly desires.

Many Christians have trouble in this area because they haven't learned to control their thoughts. A lady once told me, "It simply didn't occur to me that I needed to direct my mind and keep it healthy and positive. If ministers preached or taught about the control of our thoughts, I never heard it. One day, however, I read an article about the power of thoughts, and God convicted me. That's when I knew I needed to change my thinking."

This lady said she drove down the street of a busy city and spotted a sign, a cartoon of a car with big eyes for the front lights and tears flowing, and the words "Please help me! I need an oil change." As she passed, she thought, *I need a mind change. I don't like being the way I am, letting my mind go wherever it wants. Part of my responsibility as a child of God is to keep my thoughts healthy and strong.*

"I want to make it clear that I went to church," she said, "and I had been active for years. I knew a lot of scripture, and I even did some volunteer work at the church. But I didn't control my thoughts. Even when I sang in church, my mind jumped from subject to subject. We'd be singing about joy and grace, and I'd think about the dishes still in the sink, the unfinished laundry, or what I wanted to eat for lunch.

"I attended church and I was faithful, but I was not faithful in attending to the Word. I listened when the preachers quoted scripture. I usually followed along with my own Bible, but I didn't really think about what I was hearing or what my eyes were reading. I was doing the right things outwardly, but I wasn't thinking the right things. My mind was a mess, and I didn't know what to do about it."

When she finally said, "I need a mind change" aloud to herself, she actually pondered the words she spoke. She was like the car on the sign—she needed a change—a mind change. She needed to let the Holy Spirit direct her thoughts instead of the devil. As she prayed, she felt confident there would be a positive change.

She thought to herself, *Is there anything I am supposed to do?* She realized that if she didn't make lifestyle changes, the devil would soon make the new thinking as muddy and gunky as the old thinking was.

For the next several days, she looked up all the scriptures she could find that used the word *study* or *meditate*. She also looked up scriptures that talked about the mind or thoughts. Among them were Proverbs 23:7, Ephesians 4:23, and Psalm 119:48. She read the verses, wrote them on slips of paper, and pondered them. The more she meditated on the right things, the less trouble she had with Satan trying to control her thoughts. That's how it works with all of us: The more we focus on God, the less often the devil can defeat us. Many people would love to have her result, but they don't want to do the work. Are you willing to do your part? If you are, I can assure you God will do His.

The more we focus on God, the less often the devil can defeat us.

CHAPTER 23

Transforming Your Mind and Your Life

The apostle Paul used two interesting words in Romans 12:2: *conform*, "be not conformed to this world," and *transform*, "but be ye transformed by the renewing of your mind" for the result that you: "may prove what is that good, and acceptable, and perfect, will of God" (KJV) "[in His sight for you]" (AMP).

I asked a friend who is a Greek scholar to help me understand the difference between them. He told me the word translated *conform* referred to the outward form. For example, my outward form at age twenty was quite different from what I'll look like at age seventy. The body changes, but it was more than that. He said the Greek word carried the idea of the changes we make according to the fashion—what was in vogue at the time—much like the way our culture goes today. One year, skirt hems are above the ankle; another year, above the knee. Those things are constantly changing.

The word Paul used for being *transformed* from the world refers to the essential part of ourselves—the part that doesn't change, our identity. He was saying that if we want to worship and serve God, we must undergo a change—but not only of our outward form. The change must be inward, and it involves our personality, our mind, and our essential being. Outward fashions may change, but inner purity is always in style.

The preceding verse, Romans 12:1, exhorts us to present ourselves to God as living sacrifices. Only Christians can do that. His words are not about *becoming* believers, but about *living* as believers. This scripture challenges us to present all of our members to God for His use. That means our mind, mouth, will, emotions, eyes, ears, hands, feet—all of us.

If we want to see God's perfect will proven in our lives, we can—but we have to have our minds transformed. We have to think different thoughts and look at life differently. We have to have disciplined minds. We must begin to think in agreement with God's Word and not the devil's lies.

> If we want to see God's perfect will proven in our lives, we can—but we have to have our minds transformed.

Although God has a different plan for each one of us, one thing applies to all: We are to have inwardly transformed minds. If our minds are transformed by the Holy Spirit, we will act differently. When He began transforming my mind, I know I acted differently. Church became a place for me to celebrate and to learn with my brothers and sisters in the faith. I began to understand worship, and I became a participant rather than someone who simply went through the motions.

Does your life need to be transformed? Start by being willing to think right thoughts, and you'll see the change in yourself—and so will others around you.

CHAPTER 24

The Devil Lies

The devil lies. In fact, the devil doesn't know how to speak the truth.

"There is no truth in him," Jesus said.

> You are of your father, the devil, and it is your will to practice the lusts and gratify the desires [which are characteristic] of your father. He was a murderer from the beginning and does not stand in the truth, because there is no truth in him. When he speaks a falsehood, he speaks what is natural to him, for he is a liar [himself] and the father of lies and of all that is false (John 8:44).

Most Christians know everything the devil says is false—and yet they still listen to his evil words. Sometimes the lies seem to just pop into our minds for no apparent reason; sometimes Satan even speaks to us through other people. He puts something critical or hurtful into their minds about us, and they speak it out for us to hear. If we listen and accept what we hear, our enemy rejoices. If we listen long enough to the deceptive information we have taken in, we will find ourselves facing serious problems. Instead of listening and absorbing the untruths and satanic deceptions, you can look at what Jesus did and follow His example. After fasting for forty days in the wilderness, Satan tempted Him three times. Each time He defeated the devil by declaring, "It is written," and quoting the Word of God. No wonder the devil fled from Him (see Matthew 4:1–11). Learn the truth of God's Word, and every time Satan lies to you, quote a scripture back to him. Learn to talk back to the devil!

Too many people don't know how to use the Word to defeat Satan's lies. Many people—even Christians—don't seem to realize they can refuse to listen to that voice. Too many people don't realize the devil attacks their minds with negative or wrong thoughts. It's his nature to lie; he is out to enslave everyone.

Too many people don't realize the devil attacks their minds with negative or wrong thoughts. It's his nature to lie; he is out to enslave everyone.

I encourage people to realize they are not alone in their spiritual battles—they are not the only ones whose minds are under attack. Satan comes against everyone. His goal is to kill, steal, and destroy, but Jesus came so we could have life and enjoy it abundantly (see John 10:10). By becoming more conscious of the spiritual weapons the Lord has made available to us and learning how to use them, we can gain victory. We can break the strongholds the devil has built in our minds. The Bible tells us when we know the truth, it will free us from Satan's strongholds (see John 8:32).

Mary illustrates someone who believed Satan's lies for years. She was mistreated by her father, and by the time she was a teen, she didn't trust men. It's no wonder she and her husband faced many conflicts in their marriage. For years, Satan whispered to her that all men were alike and wanted to hurt women and take advantage of them.

As Mary read the Bible and prayed more effectively, she learned it was the devil who was pushing her around. Now she knows she can be free. As Mary develops in her relationship with God, she is equipping herself to win the battle for her mind. She's learning more about God and more about how to pray effectively.

"Jesus has become my friend," Mary said. She knew Him as her Savior and worshiped Him as God, but this friendship was a new revelation to her. One day she read Hebrews 2:18 in a totally new light. It says of Jesus, "Because He Himself [in His humanity] has suffered in being tempted (tested and tried), He is able... to run to the cry of (assist, relieve) those who are being tempted."

That passage came alive to Mary because she saw Jesus not only as God, but as her friend—One Who knows what it is to be tempted and Who knows what it is to suffer. "I knew He died on the cross, but I had not thought of all the pain He went through for me. To realize that He understands my pain and problems was a new thought to me."

Mary also says that when negative, mean, or ugly thoughts come into her head, she is learning to stop those thoughts. "Jesus wouldn't talk that way. Jesus wouldn't be critical and judgmental, so that's the devil fighting for my mind."

Mary hasn't won all the battles, but she has learned to fight the great deceiver. Every time she wins one battle, the next one becomes easier.

CHAPTER 25

Think About What You Are Thinking About

Some people are very unhappy, and they've been that way so long they no longer realize there is another option. I can well remember being like that. I blamed my unhappiness on the way others behaved. I thought my husband and children caused me the most unhappiness. If they would change and just be a little more sensitive to my needs, I knew I would feel better. If they would help around the house more, volunteer to run errands, or just ask how I was doing, I knew I would be happy. Of course, I never said anything to them. *If they were sensitive and caring,* I thought, *they would be able to see how they could help me and make my life easier.*

I did pray about it, and I often told God how much happier I would be if they cooperated more, but they didn't change.

One day, God revealed something to me—but it wasn't what I wanted to know. He impressed me with the words, *Think about what you are thinking about.* I had no idea what God meant. In fact, the words didn't make sense. How could I think about what I was thinking about?

My mind raced from one thought to another, and I realized the truth: My thoughts centered on myself and my needs. I thought that if *they—the other people in my life*—changed, I would be happy. I reluctantly admitted that even if they changed, I would find something else to be unhappy about. I was just unhappy and didn't need any particular reason. It was first one thing and then another.

As I pondered my condition, I thought of Philippians 4:8, where Paul presents a list of the kinds of things needing our focus. If God did not want me to think about the things I was thinking about, I first needed to know what I *should* think about. I soon realized I had a lot to learn. Although I had been attending church for years, I could not remember anyone ever telling me how important my thoughts were to God and to my quality of life.

If we concentrate our thoughts on good things, the kind of things Paul mentions in that verse—"Whatever is true, whatever is worthy of reverence and is honorable and seemly, whatever is just, whatever is pure, whatever is lovely and lovable, whatever is kind and winsome and gracious, if there is any virtue and excellence, if there is anything worthy of praise, think on and weigh and take account of these things [fix your minds on them]"—we will be built up. We will grow spiritually and become strong in the Lord.

As I continued to meditate on God's message, I realized how my thoughts affected my attitude—and this is true of all of us. God tells us to do things that are for our good. He wants us to be happy and fulfilled. If we want happiness and fulfillment, we must find it God's way. If we're full of wrong thoughts, we're miserable. That's not a theory—that's spoken from my own experience and is found in God's Word. I've also learned that when we're miserable, we usually end up making others around us miserable too.

> God tells us to do things that are for our good. He wants us to be happy and fulfilled.

Since those days, I've made it a practice to take a regular inventory of my thoughts. I review the way I think. *What have I been thinking about?* I ask myself.

I stress this because—as I learned from my own experience—Satan deceives us into thinking that the source of our misery or pain is other people or sometimes our situations. He tries to keep us from facing our own thoughts as the source of our unhappiness. I would venture to say that it is practically impossible to be happy while maintaining negative, critical, depressing thoughts. We need to overcome Satan's attempted deception in this area of the battle for our thoughts, and God will help us if we ask Him.

CHAPTER 26

Peace in the Night

What is it about nighttime that makes us seem more vulnerable to discouragement, fear, and negative thoughts? Is it just because it's dark? Is there some kind of association between evil and the darkness of night? We may find we are able to cope with whatever happens to us during the day, but really struggle at night.

My theory is that by evening, most of us are tired and weary, and we just want to lie down, close our eyes, and drift into peaceful sleep. Satan knows we are not as resistant to his attacks when we are exhausted and sleepy, so this becomes one of his favorite times to engage us in the battle of our minds. And just as we are about to drop off to sleep, he makes his move.

If we recognize we're more susceptible to the attack of the enemy at night, we can take steps to be better prepared to stand against him. Some of my friends tell me they find it helps to meditate on scriptures such as Philippians 4:8, which tell us to think on the good things that are true, honorable, just, pure, lovely, and excellent. Or they claim the promise of Isaiah 26:3: "You will guard him and keep him in perfect and constant peace whose mind [both its inclination and its character] is stayed on You." These words from the Bible enable us to remain vigilant even in the dark hours of night. By using the Word of God, we can defeat every onslaught of the enemy—even in our weakest hours.

By using the Word of God, we can defeat every onslaught of the enemy—even in our weakest hours.

If we have not armed ourselves with the Word and spent some

time in prayer, however, we will fall for Satan's plan when he brings to mind some troublesome event of the day, causing us to think to ourselves, *Why did I say that? How could I have been so insensitive?*

He takes advantage of us when he knows we are weak and the most vulnerable to his influence. His goal is to disturb our thoughts and rob us of the peaceful rest our bodies need. One of his tricks is to cause us to focus on the problems of the day, suggesting that we must immediately—in the middle of the night—determine the best way to settle the issue.

I experienced nights like this years ago, and I didn't always win the battle. But as a more experienced Christian, I now know how to fight the good fight of faith. Here's one thing I figured out a long time ago: It is not wise to make decisions in the middle of the night. Most decisions can wait until the next day.

Perhaps we spoke hastily or didn't respond kindly to someone's need. Someone may have spoken unkindly to us. The issues are often little things that probably could have been handled better. But as Satan wages his battle in the dark of night, those little things seem to take on importance and urgency—so much so we believe we will never sleep unless we settle the issue immediately.

When Satan tries to pull that nighttime trick on me, I've learned to say, "I'll deal with this issue in the morning, when the sun is shining. After I've rested, I can cope." I've also learned I can say, "Lord, I surrender this to You. Give me Your rest, Your peace, and help me make the right decision in the morning." That works for me!

CHAPTER 27

Control Your Wandering Thoughts

In the days when Peter wrote the words in 1 Peter 1:13, men wore long, flowing robes that hindered fast progress or strenuous action. "Wherefore gird up the loins of your mind, be sober, and hope to the end for the grace that is to be brought unto you at the revelation of Jesus Christ" (KJV). Men wore broad belts (or girdles) around their waists, and when they wanted to move into action, they "girded up their loins"—that is, they shortened their robes by pulling them up inside their belts. That phrase is similar to what we mean when we say, "Roll up your sleeves." Peter's words here are a serious call to action—a reminder that when we lose our focus, it is time for us to do some serious thinking.

If you do not discipline your mind to remain focused on what is important, the devil will cause it to wander aimlessly to other things.

Staying too busy can result in an abnormal mind as opposed to a normal mind. Another way the devil attacks your normal mind is by causing your thoughts to wander. It's a mental attack. If you do not discipline your mind to remain focused on what is important, the devil will cause it to wander aimlessly to other things.

When this inability to concentrate goes on for a while, you may begin to wonder if there is something wrong with your mind. What you often fail to realize is that when you allow your mind to wander too long it becomes a deeply rooted bad habit. In some cases, there may be physical causes for not being able to concentrate, such as anemia or certain B-vitamin deficiencies. You may not be eating properly. Or you may have become excessively fatigued. It's a good idea to consider all the potential causes as you search for a solution. I've learned that when I'm excessively tired, Satan tries to attack my mind because he knows it's more difficult for me to resist him during those times.

Sometimes a lack of concentration creates a lack of comprehension. Perhaps as you are reading the Bible, you find yourself hurrying to get through so you can do something else. Out of a sense of duty, you are determined to finish reading a chapter—and you do. But when you are finished, you can't recall anything you read. Your eyes scanned the pages, but your mind was engaged somewhere else.

Perhaps you have even experienced this battle for your mind in church. You attend regularly—the devil hasn't been able to stop that—but he still causes your mind to wander during the sermon. Have you ever been fully engrossed in listening to a sermon, and then you suddenly realize your mind has wandered and you have no idea what was said?

If the devil can rob you of the benefits of reading the Bible and hearing God's Word at church, he has won some major skirmishes in the battle for your mind. This is why Peter says to "gird up the loins of your mind." You must take action by confronting your wandering mind and disciplining it to focus on what is important.

In conversation, I used to fake it when I realized my mind had wandered. Now I deal with it honestly and when it is appropriate I ask, "Would you please back up and repeat that? I let my mind wander off, and I didn't hear a thing you said." This kind of behavior not only interrupts the plan of the enemy but also brings victory over the problem.

It's not easy to discipline your mind when it has been allowed to wander aimlessly, but you can do it. When you discover your thoughts have wandered, you must exercise discipline and make the necessary corrections. The devil would like to convince you that you can't help yourself, but when you consistently come against his bid for your mind, he is defeated, and you have won another battle.

CHAPTER 28

The Time-Waster of Wondering

When you say the words, "I wonder," they sound innocent and honest. They also represent the way we avoid certainty and making decisions.

Suppose you're the CEO of a business. Every day twenty people come to your office and ask you to make decisions. Yours is the final answer on everything that goes on in the corporation. Instead of giving decisive answers, you rub your chin, stare out the window, and say, "I wonder. I wonder what we should do about that."

An indecisive CEO wouldn't stay in that position very long. The position is much too important to the overall success and well-being of the organization and all associated with it. You are not in that position to wonder—you're there to act.

Many of us forget this is the way it is with the Christian life as well. Often, instead of choosing what we need to do, we avoid facing the situation by saying, "I wonder." I know because I've done it. In times past, when I've been invited to a party or to be the featured speaker at a banquet, I've said, "I wonder what I should wear." It's easy for me to waste a lot of time looking through my closet, considering the color and style, as I try to choose just the right outfit for a particular occasion.

This may seem like such a small thing—and it really is. The problem, however, is that if we allow enough of these wonderings in our lives, not only do we fail to accomplish the things we need to do, but wondering becomes the normal way our minds function and we waste a lot of time. Being indecisive keeps us from moving forward and can eventually defeat us.

> Being indecisive keeps us from moving forward and can eventually defeat us.

God's Word clearly teaches us to be decisive. I asked a friend where she wanted to eat lunch and she asked, "What are my options?" As soon as I told her she thought for a few seconds and made a decision. We should know our options and then make decisions. Wondering keeps us floating between two or more things and never settling on anything. It is quite frustrating not only to us but, perhaps even more so, to other people involved with us. It is fine to ponder an issue for a reasonable amount of time. I am not suggesting we make rash decisions without giving them proper thought. But I am trying to be very clear about the total waste of "wondering."

Know what you want God to do and ask Him to do it! Sometimes God's people are reluctant to ask boldly for big things, but Jesus has given us permission to step out in faith and ask boldly. And yet some still waste time just wondering. They wonder what it would be like if God would give them a better job. They wonder what it would be like if God would give them a larger house. Don't wonder... ASK!

So stop wondering and start acting! That's one of the most important things I've learned about the wondering mind. Rather than wondering what I should wear to a banquet, I look at my clothes and I decide. God gave me the ability to make wise choices, so I can just do it instead of wasting my time wondering.

Wondering and indecision can become strongholds in our minds that can leave us feeling confused, insecure, and ineffective. But that's not God's plan. He wants us to overcome the wondering thoughts by believing then receiving the answer to our prayers from God, by faith.

Jesus did not say, "Whatever things you wonder when you pray, you will have." Instead, He said, "Whatever you ask for in prayer, believe (trust and be confident) that it is granted to you, and you will [get it]" (Mark 11:24).

CHAPTER 29

Double-Minded and Confused

My friend Eva received a summons for jury duty in a robbery trial. For two days, twelve citizens listened to the prosecuting attorney as he presented evidence to indicate the accused had broken into a home and stolen many items. Eva was ready to convict him.

On the third day, the defense attorney presented the other side of the picture. The more Eva listened, the more confused she became. What once seemed very obvious now seemed ambiguous and contradictory. Although the jury did convict the man, Eva said she struggled over making the right decision. Each attorney, when he was speaking, seemed to be the most convincing.

Many Christians live much the same way day to day. They have become what James calls double-minded.

> If any of you is deficient in wisdom, let him ask of the giving God [Who gives] to everyone liberally and ungrudgingly, without reproaching or faultfinding, and it will be given him. Only it must be in faith that he asks with no wavering (no hesitating, no doubting). For the one who wavers (hesitates, doubts) is like the billowing surge out at sea that is blown hither and thither and tossed by the wind (James 1:5–6).
>
> For let not that man think that he shall receive any thing of the Lord. A double minded man is unstable in all his ways (vv. 7–8 KJV).

They're sure of one thing until something else happens, and then they flip-flop opinions. In their double-mindedness, they flit from one opinion to the other. They're sure they know what to do, and then they switch again. The moment they feel sure they have made the decision they plan to stick with, they begin to wonder if it was the correct one. They continually doubt and question their reasoning.

This kind of behavior is not the same as being open-minded. To be open-minded means being willing to hear all sides of an issue—like jurors should be at a trial. But eventually we have to sort through the evidence or the circumstances in life and say, "This is what I'm going to do."

That sounds good, but too many people have trouble being decisive. "What if I make a mistake?" they ask. "What if I choose the wrong thing?" Those are legitimate questions, but they are not meant to paralyze God's people and prevent them from acting. Too often, these are tools Satan uses to distract and prevent Christians from taking action.

I'm an expert on this. For many years, I was that double-minded person James wrote about. I didn't like being that way. It took so much energy to keep rethinking the same problems. But I was so afraid of making a mistake I didn't know how to make good decisions. It took a long time before I realized the devil had declared war against me, and my mind was his personal battlefield. At that moment of awareness, I felt totally confused about everything but I didn't understand why.

Many of God's people are living exactly where I was then. They're reasonable people. That is, they have the ability to figure out causes and reasons. They sincerely try to understand all the implications of a situation and find the most sensible or logical solution by putting their reasoning ability to work. This is often the opportunity Satan takes to sneak in and steal the will of God from them. God may speak to them about doing a certain thing, and it may not always seem to be the most sensible course of action. This presents an opportunity for the devil to cause them to question—to become double-minded. The Amplified Bible says the mind of the flesh is "sense and reason without the Holy Spirit" (Romans 8:6). I am not suggesting that you pay no attention to common sense and reason, but if we are not also listening to the Holy Spirit we will become unbalanced and *our reasoning becomes unreasonable.*

For example, sometimes I sense God wants me to bless people by giving to them—often an item of jewelry or clothing. On one occasion I remember, God wanted me to give away a new and fairly expensive dress I had never worn. It didn't make sense when I went through the natural reasoning process, but when I checked my heart to see what I felt God was saying, I had the assurance it was indeed the right thing to do. God is not always reasonable!

Ask of the One Who gives wisdom liberally, and He will free you from being indecisive and double-minded.

God's Spirit is always available to free you from natural reasoning that leaves you confused. Ask of the One Who gives wisdom liberally, and He will free you from being indecisive and double-minded.

CHAPTER 30

Holy Fear

At the time Jehoshaphat became king, Judah was a small nation, and the surrounding nations could easily defeat them. We learn that, after seeking the advice of a prophet, the king reformed his kingdom to be in alignment with God (see 2 Chronicles 18:19). Following Jehoshaphat's actions, "the Moabites, the Ammonites, and with them the Meunites came against Jehoshaphat to battle" (2 Chronicles 20:1).

The most "sensible" thing would have been for the king to surrender and forge some kind of treaty. There was no human way such a small nation could defeat such large armies. In that context, we read that the king was afraid—and why wouldn't he be? But he didn't stop with fear.

I want to make this point clear. To feel fear isn't sin or failure or disobedience. In fact, some fear is a warning to us. It's a shout of danger. But then we must decide what to do with the fear. We can act; we can cringe; we can ignore it. King Jehoshaphat did the right thing: He "set himself [determinedly, as his vital need] to seek the Lord" (v. 3). He didn't have answers, and he certainly wasn't stupid enough to think that his tiny army could defeat his enemies. And that's an important lesson for us to learn in our battles against Satan. Our enemy is powerful, and if we think we can defeat him by ourselves, we're foolish and badly mistaken.

The king not only prayed, but he also proclaimed a fast throughout the entire land. The Bible goes on to say he stood in the midst of the people and prayed for deliverance: "For we have no might to stand against this great company that is coming against us. We do not know what to do, but our eyes are upon You" (v. 12).

That is exactly the prayer God wanted to hear. The people admitted they didn't know what to do, that they couldn't win, and their only hope was in God's deliverance. Just then, the Holy Spirit came upon a man named Jahaziel. "He said, hearken, all Judah, you inhabitants of Jerusalem, and you King Jehoshaphat. The Lord says this to you: Be not afraid or dismayed at this great multitude; for the battle is not yours, but God's" (v. 15). He went on to say, "You shall not need to fight in this battle; take your positions, stand still, and see the deliverance of the Lord [Who is] with you.... Fear not nor be dismayed" (v. 17). The account goes on to say the people began to sing praises to God. When they did that, God had warriors from Mount Seir sneak in and kill Judah's enemies so that none escaped.

A good fear is to be afraid to try to handle your problems on your own and to immediately cry out to God.

That's the biggest secret of winning the battles against your enemy. Acknowledge your fear—then let it push you to seek God. A good fear is to be afraid to try to handle your problems on your own and to immediately cry out to God.

When you cry out in holy fear, God hears and races to your rescue. That's His promise, and He never breaks His promises.

CHAPTER 31

Fear Not!

Wouldn't everything in life be better if we didn't have to deal with fear? Of course, there are healthy fears that alert us to danger—and these are good because they protect us. There is also the fear of God, which means to have a holy, reverential awe and respect for Him. But there is a debilitating fear Satan tries to put on us every day intended to keep us from having the power, love, and sound mind God wants us to have.

If you have ever struggled as I once did with anxiety, you are familiar with the worry, stress, and feeling of heaviness that comes with it. Many people struggle with fear that has no obvious cause or source. They wonder why they are always afraid and can't change, no matter how hard they try. Others spend every minute worrying about what might happen. "What if..." is their favorite phrase. "What if I can't pay the bills?" "What if my child gets hurt?" "What if my husband loses his job?" The endless list of possible tragedies keeps these unfortunate people bound up and miserable every day of their lives.

There are many serious things going on in the world, and we need to be aware of them and prepare for them. But we also need to learn to resist fear when it arises against us. The Word tells us, "God did not give us a spirit of timidity (of cowardice, of craven and cringing and fawning fear), but [He has given us a spirit] of power and of love and of calm and well-balanced mind and discipline and self-control" (2 Timothy 1:7).

Sometimes we think of fear as an emotion, but we need to realize that fear is actually a spirit. In fact, I believe fear is one of Satan's favorite tools, and he particularly loves to torment Christians with it. At every possible opportunity, he will whisper in your ear, telling you God has forgotten you and there is no hope. It makes sense that Satan would try to intimidate us with fear.

But Jesus said, "All things can be (are possible) to him who believes!" (Mark 9:23). We have to believe there is nothing worse for the enemy than an on-fire, Bible-believing, fearless Christian! God didn't promise us life would be easy. We will all face problems and challenges. But the outcome depends on whether we trust God—or give in to fear.

Psalm 23:4 says, "Yes, though I walk through the [deep, sunless] valley of the shadow of death, I will fear or dread no evil, for You are with me." The psalmist David said he *walked* through the valley.

When we become afraid, we can be sure it is not God at work, but one of the sly tricks of our spiritual enemy. If he can make us think God won't come through for us, or is angry at us, or wants to punish us, we allow those thoughts to fill our minds, and we start losing the battle.

God is love.

> There is no fear in love [dread does not exist], but full-grown (complete, perfect) love turns fear out of doors and expels every trace of terror! (1 John 4:18).
>
> But God shows and clearly proves His [own] love for us by the fact that while we were still sinners, Christ (the Messiah, the Anointed one) died for us (Romans 5:8).

> A courageous person is not one who never feels fear, but someone who feels fear and takes proper action anyway.

We can never say those words enough. The only thing we can add is: God is love, and God loves me! Fear is a spirit that must be confronted head-on—it will not leave on its own. We can take positive action even in the presence of the feeling of fear. Actually a courageous person is not one who never feels fear, but someone who feels fear and takes proper action anyway. We must proclaim the Word of God and let fear know that it is not going to rule us. So the next time fear knocks on your door, send faith to answer!

CHAPTER 32

When Someone Fails

As a believer in Jesus one of the things you will have to learn to deal with is other people's faults and failures. What should your attitude be?

Paul instructed people not to teach others to do things they were not doing themselves:

> Well then, you who teach others, do you not teach yourself? While you teach against stealing, do you steal (take what does not really belong to you)? You who say not to commit adultery, do you commit adultery [are you unchaste in action or in thought]? . . . You who boast in the Law, do you dishonor God by breaking the Law [by stealthily infringing upon or carelessly neglecting or openly breaking it]? (Romans 2:21–23).

It is confusing for a young Christian if or when they see church leaders or those in authority doing things they know aren't right. It can either lead them to be discouraged and give up or cause them to think, *If you can act that way and still be a Christian then I guess I can too.* We each need to remember that God has called us to be responsible for our actions. Don't use someone else's bad behavior as an excuse to behave badly yourself. God holds us accountable for every thought and every action—but our responsibility doesn't stop there. We are also responsible to help lift up others when they fall. We would like to see those who lead or teach

Don't use someone else's bad behavior as an excuse to behave badly yourself.

others always live up to what they teach, but the truth is we all make mistakes.

Perhaps nowhere in the Bible is this concept more clearly defined than in Galatians 6:1–3. Paul lays down three important principles Satan doesn't want us to grasp. First, when we become aware a sister or brother has fallen into sin, we are to do whatever we can to help lift up that person. Paul writes,

> If any person is overtaken in misconduct or sin of any sort, you who are spiritual [who are responsive to and controlled by the Spirit] should set him right and restore and reinstate him, without any sense of superiority and with all gentleness, keeping an attentive eye on yourself, lest you should be tempted also. Bear (endure, carry) one another's burdens and troublesome moral faults, and in this way fulfill and observe perfectly the law of Christ (the Messiah) and complete what is lacking [in your obedience to it]. For if any person thinks himself to be somebody [too important to condescend to shoulder another's load] when he is nobody [of superiority except in his own estimation], he deceives and deludes and cheats himself.

Even the best of us fail at times, but it is important to note that the word *overtaken* doesn't mean a deliberate, intentional sin. It's as if someone is walking down an icy sidewalk, slips, and falls. That's how the Christian life works—nearly everyone slips sometimes.

What then should be our attitude when this happens? We should offer to help, of course. If someone slips on the ice, don't you naturally rush over to help that person get up? We would not ignore a person like that, nor should we ignore the responsibility to help those who have slipped spiritually. One of the biggest ways we can help is to pray instead of gossiping or judging.

The Greek word translated "restore" (v. 1) was once a medical term used by a surgeon to describe medical procedures like removing a growth from a body or setting a broken arm. The goal is not to see the person punished, but the person healed.

The second point Paul made is, instead of pointing fingers and looking down on someone when we become aware the person has fallen, we should look at ourselves. The devil could have tempted us to do the same thing or something else just as bad, or even worse. We need to look with compassion on those who fall and remind ourselves, "Except for the grace of God, I could be there."

The third thing is to push away pride in our own achievements. If we think we are more spiritual, we're deceiving ourselves. Proverbs 16:18 gives this warning: "Pride goes before destruction, and a haughty spirit before a fall." It is pretty dangerous to say, "I would never do that!" We need to pray that we will always be strong and faithful, but bragging is a dangerous thing. When we see other people make mistakes we need to ask ourselves, "What would Jesus do in this situation?" and if we find ourselves in that same situation, then we should respond the way we truly believe He would.

CHAPTER 33

Suspicious of Suspicion

The words about love in 1 Corinthians 13:4–8 are familiar to most of us, but I can honestly say living them has not always been easy for me. These are the attributes of love: enduring long, being patient and kind, and not being envious, jealous, boastful, vain, or rude. Love doesn't act unbecomingly or insist on its own rights or its own way, for it isn't self-seeking. It isn't touchy or easily provoked; it doesn't take account of the evil done to it or rejoice at injustice. It rejoices in the truth, bears up under everything that comes, is ever ready to believe the best of every person, has fadeless hopes, and never fails.

As a child, I was not exposed to this kind of love—in fact, I was taught to be suspicious of everyone. I was told the motives of other people were not to be trusted. As I became older, I encountered people whose actions confirmed in my mind that my suspicions were justified. Even as a young Christian, I experienced disappointment because of the obvious motives of some people in the church. While it is wise to be aware of people's motives, we must be careful we don't allow a suspicious nature to negatively affect our feelings about everyone.

An overly suspicious nature can poison your mind and affect your ability to love and accept other people. Consider this example. Suppose a friend approaches you after a church service and says, "Do you know what Doris thinks about you?" Then this friend tells you every detail of the things Doris said. The first problem is a true friend wouldn't share such information. And the second problem is that with an already suspicious mind, you now believe secondhand information without even giving the accused an opportunity to share their side of the story.

Once your mind has been poisoned against someone, suspicion grows. Satan gains a stronghold in your mind. Every time Doris says something to you, you are automatically suspicious, thinking, *What does she really mean?* Or if she's nice to you, you think, *I wonder what she wants from me.*

This is the way Satan works. If he can make you suspicious of others, it isn't long before you don't trust anything they say. And if you've been hurt like this several times, the devil can poison your thinking to the point you start wondering who else may be talking about you behind your back.

Let's continue the example. Suppose that one day in church, Doris is sitting just a few rows in front of you, clapping her hands and praising the Lord. Immediately you think, *She's such a hypocrite.* Unless you make a decision to believe the best, the devil will keep filling your mind with suspicious thoughts until you are literally tormented not only about Doris but about many others as well.

Our ministry encountered a very hurtful situation once. A man we knew for over twenty-five years and who we considered to be a trusted friend was caught stealing from us. The first thing I thought was, *Well, I guess you just cannot trust anybody!* Satan used the wound I had to try and poison my attitude toward everyone, but thankfully I knew not to let that negative, suspicious attitude take root in my heart. I actually stopped and prayed, "Lord, I will not allow myself to be cynical and have a suspicious attitude. Help me deal with this properly and not let it affect my future."

> Unless you make a decision to believe the best, the devil will keep filling your mind with suspicious thoughts until you are literally tormented.

The world is filled with distrust and suspicion, and I encourage you to not ever let yourself be part of that way of thinking. The Bible says love always believes the best of every person!

CHAPTER 34

Passive or Passionate?

The apostle Paul said, "Leave no [such] room or foothold for the devil [give no opportunity to him]" (Ephesians 4:27). Perhaps the best way to summarize these words is: When the devil knocks on the door, don't open it and invite him in. There are many ways we actually give the devil an opening to pounce on us. One of those ways involves being passive.

To be passive is the opposite of being active. This can be a dangerous problem because it means you aren't on guard or aren't actively standing up, and you aren't alert. One of the devil's most deceitful tricks is to get you to do nothing and to feel content about it.

I have found a wide variety of definitions for the word *passive*, but I describe it as a lack of feeling, a lack of desire, apathy, laziness, and lukewarmness. It is what John referred to when he wrote to the church at Laodicea: "I know your [record of] works and what you are doing; you are neither cold nor hot. Would that you were cold or hot!" (Revelation 3:15).

That statement reminds me of something someone told me years ago. "I've been a good Christian today," he said. "I haven't hurt anyone or done anyone any harm." In a moment of insight, I said, "But have you done any good for anyone?" He stared at me for several seconds before he said, "I guess I never thought of it that way. I was so concerned about not doing anything wrong, that I never thought about doing anything good."

This illustrates one of the tricks the devil plays on our minds. All we need to do is read the Bible to find out what God says. Paul wrote

Timothy to stir up the gift of God in him (see 2 Timothy 1:6–7). Paul told his young disciple to shake himself up and do something—which is good for us to consider as well. This passage urges us to get moving and start using the gifts God has given us. Timothy was becoming fearful and Paul told him to get stirred up because fear was not God's will for him.

The devil knows inactivity, laziness, or failure to exercise our will for doing good can throw us into ultimate defeat. As long as we take action against the devil, we can win the battle. When we do nothing, we are on dangerous ground. When we are stirred into action, passionate about faith, and zealous to follow God, we can destroy all the devil's influence.

Peter wrote to the persecuted believers of his day to be well balanced—meaning temperate, sober of mind—and at all times vigilant and cautious. He warned them the devil prowls around like a roaring lion looking for someone to devour, and to resist him, firm in their faith (see 1 Peter 5:8–9). I emphasize this because I see many believers who don't feel passionate about anything, so they don't do anything. They attend worship services and praise the Lord if they feel like it. They read their Bibles if they have the energy and time. If they don't feel like doing something, they just don't do it. They don't finish what they start.

> When we are stirred into action, passionate about faith, and zealous to follow God, we can destroy all the devil's influence.

That's not God's way. We need to stir ourselves up—the way Paul urged Timothy. I'll use myself as an example to illustrate what I mean. I always intensely disliked physical exercise, so I never did much of it. God convicted me that I really needed to get on a good exercise program if I wanted to be strong for the rest of my journey here on earth. It was a hard decision for me to make, but once I got started I learned that I actually really liked it. Now I look forward to it and am really disappointed if for any reason I have to miss one of my sessions. When I first started I ached all over. Because I had been so inactive (passive) for so long, the physical exercise was painful! If you are accustomed to being passive and inactive in your spiritual life, it may be difficult to begin, but once you do you will like the results you see.

Let me encourage you to stir yourself up. Get active. You don't want to give place to the devil by doing nothing. If you make the effort to praise God and to read the Bible, you give God the opportunity to bless you. If you don't make the effort, you are inviting the enemy into your life. Get moving! Start today. You have hundreds of joints in your body and God gave them to you because He expects you to move!

CHAPTER 35

The Mind of Christ

First Corinthians 2:16 tells us we have the mind of Christ. This statement overwhelms many people. If these were not the words of the Bible, they wouldn't believe it. As it is, most people shake their heads and ask, "How can this be?"

Paul was not saying we're perfect or we'll never fail. He was telling us, as believers in Jesus, the Son of God, we are given the mind of Christ. That is, we can think spiritual thoughts because Christ is alive within us. We no longer have to think the way we once did. We can begin to think as He did.

Another way to look at this is to point to the promise God spoke through Ezekiel: "A new heart will I give you and a new spirit will I put within you, and I will take away the stony heart out of your flesh and give you a heart of flesh. And I will put my Spirit within you" (Ezekiel 36:26–27).

God gave that promise through the prophet when the Jews were in exile in Babylon. He wanted to show them their present situation was not the end. They had sinned and failed Him in every conceivable way, but He would not abandon them. Instead, He would change them. He would give them a new spirit—His Holy Spirit.

When we have the Holy Spirit living and active within us, the mind of Christ is in action. The mind of Christ is given to us to direct us in the right way. If we have His mind, we will think positive thoughts. We will think about how blessed we are—how good God has been to us. I am not sure enough can ever be said about the power of being positive and looking at things the way God sees them.

Jesus was positive—in spite of facing a multitude of negative experiences that include being lied about, lonely, misunderstood, and deserted by His disciples when He needed them most—and was always able to offer an uplifting, encouraging word. Just being in His presence would suggest that all fear, negative thoughts, and discouraging hopelessness would evaporate into thin air.

The mind of Christ in us is positive. So when we fall for the opportunity to be negative about something, we should instantly discern that we are not operating with the mind of Christ. God wants us to be lifted up. It's the enemy of our soul who wants us pressed down—depressed. Except for a medical reason, I do not think it is possible to be depressed without being negative. We have many opportunities to think negative thoughts, but that is not the mind of Christ at work in us. We don't have to accept those thoughts. They are not His!

> We have many opportunities to think negative thoughts, but that is not the mind of Christ at work in us. We don't have to accept those thoughts. They are not His!

Every situation gives us an opportunity to make a choice. It is obvious, of course, we can choose the good or the bad. What we often forget is that we choose the bad or the wrong without conscious thought. We follow old patterns—or the old mind—and not the mind of Christ. As God promised the Jews through Ezekiel's prophecy, He will give us a new heart and a new spirit, but we still have the power to choose which mind—the mind of the flesh out of habit or the mind of Christ—we want to follow.

CHAPTER 36

Meditate on These Things

Transcendental Meditation. Yoga. New Age. Eastern Religions. Hearing these terms causes many Christians to fear the word *meditation* so much they never realize it was God's idea first. They're afraid if they meditate they will be part of the occult or some type of pagan worship. What we need to remember is how often the Bible urges us to meditate.

It is not meditation that is wrong; it is what one meditates on that could be wrong. We can explain biblical meditation in a number of ways, but the one I find most helpful is to think of it as expressed in the Bible. If we read verses such as Psalm 63:5–6, "My mouth shall praise You with joyful lips when I remember You upon my bed and meditate on You in the night watches," and Psalm 119:97, "Oh, how love I Your law! It is my meditation all the day," among many others, we see three significant things about meditation in the Word.

First, the Scriptures refer to more than a quick reading or pausing for a few brief, reflecting thoughts. The Bible presents meditation as serious pondering. Whenever the Bible refers to meditation, it speaks to serious, committed followers. This isn't a word for quick, pick-me-up Bible verses or Precious Promises. I'm not opposed to those, but this is a call to deeper, more serious concentration.

Second, the biblical contexts show meditation as ongoing and habitual: "It is my meditation all the day." God told Joshua to meditate on the law day and night (see Joshua 1:8). Psalm 1:2 says that the godly person meditates on God's law day and night. The Scriptures give us the impression the people who spoke of meditating did so very seriously and fully applied their minds to it.

Third, meditation has a reward. It's not just to meditate or go through a religious ritual. In most of the biblical passages where the term occurs, the writer goes on to point out the results. Again in Joshua 1:8: "For then you shall make your way prosperous, and then you shall deal wisely and have good success." Psalm 1 describes the godly person who meditates day and night on God's law (or Word): "And everything he does shall prosper [and come to maturity]" (v. 3).

Despite what I've pointed out, we don't talk or teach very much about meditation today. It's hard work! It demands time. Meditation also demands discipline and undivided attention.

If you want to win the battle for the mind, meditation is a powerful weapon for you to use. You must focus on portions of God's Word. You must read them, perhaps repeat them aloud, and keep them before you. Some people repeat a verse again and again until the meaning fills their mind and becomes part of their thinking. The idea is that you won't put the Word of God in practice physically until you first practice it mentally. Meditation is a life principle because it ministers life to you, and your behavior ministers life to others through you.

> You won't put the Word of God in practice physically until you first practice it mentally.

I could go on and on about the subject of meditating on God's Word, because it seems there is no end to what God can show me out of one verse of scripture. The Word of God is a treasure chest of powerful, life-giving secrets God wants to reveal to us. I believe these truths are manifested to those who meditate on, ponder, study, think about, practice mentally, and mutter the Word of God. The Lord reveals Himself to us when we diligently meditate on His Word. Throughout the day, as you go about your affairs, ask the Holy Spirit to remind you of certain scriptures on which you can meditate.

You'll be amazed at how much power will be released into your life from this practice. The more you meditate on God's Word, the more you will be able to draw readily upon its strength in times of trouble.

This is how we can stay filled with the Holy Spirit—stay with the Lord through meditation and through singing and praising. As we spend time in His Presence and ponder His Word, we grow, we encourage others, and we win the battles against the enemy of our minds.

CHAPTER 37

The Blessings of Meditation

God not only frequently tells us to meditate—to ponder seriously—His Word, but He frequently promises results. It's as if God says, "Okay, Joyce, if you meditate, here's what I'm going to do for you." The writer of Proverbs 4:20–22 used the words "attend to my words" which is another way of exhorting us to meditate. "My son, attend to my words; consent and submit to my sayings. Let them not depart from your sight; keep them in the center of your heart. For they are life to those who find them, healing and health to all their flesh."

In this passage, the promise is life and health. Isn't that amazing? It's even a promise that contemplating and brooding over the Bible will affect your physical body.

We've known for a long time that filling our minds with healthy, positive thoughts affects our body and improves our health. This is just another way of repeating this truth. Or take the opposite viewpoint: Suppose we fill our minds with negative thoughts and remind ourselves how frail we are or how sick we were the day before. We soon become so filled with self-pity and self-defeating thoughts we get even sicker. Why not look at it like this: "I'm going to think about something, so it might as well be the Word of God because it is full of life and power"?

Psalm 1 and Joshua 1:8 tell us that prosperity will come from meditating on the Word. I believe by prosperity God means we will be enriched and prosper in every part of our lives. It isn't a promise of mere material wealth, but an assurance of being able to enjoy all the wonderful blessings we have.

We often forget God wants our fellowship, our company, and our time with Him. If we want a deep relationship with our heavenly Father, we have to make room for time with God. We all want special times with God, but they won't happen if we never make time for them.

> We all want special times with God, but they won't happen if we never make time for them.

D. L. Moody once said the Bible would keep us from sin, or sin would keep us from the Bible. That's the principle here. As we concentrate on God's Word and allow it to fill our thoughts, we will push away all desire to sin or to displease God in any way. We become more deeply rooted in Him. Again, think of it in the negative. When our minds remain focused on our problems, we become consumed with them. If we meditate on what's wrong with others, we see even more flaws and faults. If what we concentrate on becomes bigger to us then just imagine how big God and His promises will become as we meditate on them. They will become so big they will crowd out everything trying to destroy us.

No matter which translation or paraphrase of Philippians 4:8 we read, the statement and message in it is powerful and describes exactly what we need to do to condition our minds for victory. Here's Eugene Peterson's paraphrase in The Message: "Summing it all up, friends, I'd say you'll do best by filling your minds and meditating on things true, noble, reputable, authentic, compelling, gracious—the best, not the worst; the beautiful, not the ugly; things to praise, not things to curse."

CHAPTER 38

Truth in the Inner Being

King David sinned with Bathsheba by having sex with her and then he even went so far as to have her husband murdered to cover his sin. He married Bathsheba and tried to ignore his sin for a year. God sent Nathan the prophet to confront him and one of the things he said was, "God desires truth in the inner being" (see Psalm 51:6). It is vital for us to be truthful with ourselves, with God, and with others. Only the truth can set us free.

God's Word is truth, and when we love it and obey it we are set free from bondages that have held us captive. David was miserable even though he was trying to ignore the real reason why. Many people blame their misery on everything and everyone, and some never get around to facing the truth that they are simply disobeying and ignoring God.

Don't ever be afraid of truth. It brings light into your life and dispels darkness. Don't be afraid of the light. True, it is a little difficult to look at if one has been in the dark a long time, but we adjust quickly and realize it is much better to live in the light than it is to live in the dark. The Holy Spirit is given to us after we receive Jesus as our Savior, so He can consistently teach us and reveal truth to us. It is an ongoing process in our lives and one that can and should be exciting. God never shows us anything wrong with us for the purpose of making us feel bad, but

> God never shows us anything wrong with us for the purpose of making us feel bad, but He wants to deliver us and make our lives better.

He wants to deliver us and make our lives better. In order to do that, we must see and accept the truth, be sorry for our sins, and be willing to turn away from the dark to the light.

Anything we hide has authority over us, but the moment we bring it out into the light it is exposed and loses its power. We instantly feel that a huge burden has lifted and our lives are made better. Yes, it is a little embarrassing to really face the things we have previously kept hidden, but it is the only pathway to freedom.

I had to face a lot of truth in order to get from where I started to where I am now. I had to face the fact that my parents really never did know how to love me properly and never would. I had to see that I allowed myself to be filled with self-pity and blame and it was not doing me or anyone else any good. I had to face the truth that I was very bitter and resentful and it was not the will of God. He actually required that I forgive all the people who were responsible for my pain and pray for them. I had to face many unpleasant things about myself and my behavior. Although I had reasons for acting and feeling the way I did, I had no right to remain that way because God was willing to heal me and set me free. All I had to do was face the truth He was showing me and depend on Him to help me change.

What has God been trying to reveal to you? Have you been hiding in the dark? If so, I urge you to come out into the light and begin your journey of total healing.

Your Will

CHAPTER 39

Making Right Choices

Making right choices is very important because life is made up of a series of choices. Sometimes we like to blame everything on the devil, but the devil cannot run our lives if we are diligent to be obedient to God.

Satan places pressure on us and he tries very hard to lead us into disobedience. The spirit wants to do what is right, but the flesh says, "I want my own way." God speaks something to your spirit, some good thing to do, and the soul says, "Now wait a minute. Let me tell you what I think. Let me tell you how I feel about that. I don't know if I feel like doing that. Let me tell you what I want." I call this ongoing commentary of the soul "I want, I think, I feel."

Underlying everything we do is the soul saying, "Let me do what I want. Let me do what I think. Let me do what I feel. I want, I think, I feel." As believers, we need to go deeper than allowing our thoughts and emotions to control us. Luke 5 has a wonderful verse in it that says to come on out in the deep and get ready for a haul (see v. 4).

Some people will never spend the inheritance Jesus died to give them because they are not living deep enough. What level are you? Are you living only on the emotional or mental level? Do you always strive to get what you want, or have you turned your will over to

God? Some people never move beyond living from their own minds. They never move beyond living based on how they feel. If they feel like going to church, they go; if they don't, they don't. If they feel like spending money, they do whether they have it or not. If they feel like cleaning house, they do; if they don't, they don't. If they feel like being kind and loving, they are; and if they don't feel like it, they are grumpy and selfish. Anyone who lives according to feelings is sowing seeds for destruction. We will always have feelings, but we must learn not to bow down to them and obey them. Our souls tell us what we want, what we think, and what we feel, not what God wants, thinks, and feels. It is very important for us to learn to divide soul and spirit, and only the Word of God can teach us how to do that (see Hebrews 4:12).

It is very important for us to learn to divide soul and spirit, and only the Word of God can teach us how to do that.

The Bible says God has set before us life and death, the blessings and the curses; therefore, choose life, that you and your descendants may live (see Deuteronomy 30:19). It is like a multiple-choice test with the answers right in front of us. Set before us is: (a) life (b) death. Choose life. We don't even have to try to figure this one out. God gave us the answer, but there are multitudes of people still failing that test every day. I encourage you to choose life!

CHAPTER 40

Just Obey

Many non-Christians don't really understand the Gospel. This isn't a new thing unique to our day. When Paul wrote to the Corinthians, he pointed out that the Greeks in his day thought it was foolish (see 1 Corinthians 2:14), and to the natural mind, it is. God sent Jesus, the sinless One, to earth for the express purpose of dying for wicked, sinful people. To unbelievers, that is foolish. The natural man cannot understand the power of the Gospel—it can only be "spiritually discerned."

This is just as true in daily living. Sometimes God speaks to us, and if we try to explain it to people who don't know Jesus, it doesn't make sense. For example, I remember one couple who went to Africa as missionaries. They had no denomination or large church behind them providing support. They sold everything they owned, including their wedding rings.

"Your wedding rings?" a skeptical relative asked. "You mean God wouldn't provide for you, so you had to do it yourself?"

The wife smiled. "No, I think we had to decide if comfort and having things like everyone else was more important than serving Jesus." The couple never doubted they were doing the right thing, but it never made sense to the skeptical relative.

It is difficult for many people to hear God speak and to obey without question. But Jesus did just that—and not only on the cross. John 4 relates the story of Jesus and the Samaritan woman at the well. What most modern readers don't get is the introduction to the story: "It was necessary for Him to go through Samaria" (v. 4). Jesus had been in

Jerusalem, and He wanted to go north to Galilee. The country of the Samaritans was in between, but Jesus didn't have to take the route passing that way. He could have taken another route and avoided going through Samaria. Most Jews avoided going through Samaria because they hated the Samaritans for mixing and marrying with people from other nations.

But Jesus went, even though it wasn't what we would have called the normal or reasonable thing to do. He went because there was a woman—and eventually a whole village—who needed to hear the message only He could deliver.

The natural people—those whose minds have not been enlightened by the Holy Spirit—scoff at us. What we do doesn't always seem logical to them. But then, who says our actions have to be logical? The Bible tells us the natural or carnal mind doesn't understand spiritual things (see 1 Corinthians 2:14). Too often, we push aside thoughts, saying, "This doesn't make any sense," and we actually ignore divine guidance. It's true, of course, the devil can flood our minds with wild thoughts that we do need to ignore, but if we pray and open ourselves to the Spirit, we soon know the difference.

Consider the story of Peter who fished all night and caught nothing. Jesus, a carpenter, came along and told him, a professional fisherman, "Put out into the deep [water], and lower your nets for a haul" (Luke 5:4).

Peter reasoned with Jesus, reminding Him they worked all night and caught nothing. But to his credit, Peter, exhausted from a long and unsuccessful night's work, heard the Lord. I'll emphasize it again: Peter heard the Lord and said, "But on the ground of Your word, I will lower the nets [again]" (v. 5). And Peter was not disappointed. They caught so many fish the nets almost broke.

This is an important principle of obedience we must grasp: obeying instead of reasoning, or as one of my friends calls it, "The Nevertheless Principle." She says sometimes she feels God leading her to do things that don't always make a lot of sense. When she hears herself expressing that sentiment, she quickly adds, "Nevertheless." Then she obeys. That is really all God asks of us: to obey instead of reasoning against something He is telling us to do. The best policy is to check with your spirit and see if you have peace rather than checking with your mind to see if what God is asking is reasonable.

> The best policy is to check with your spirit and see if you have peace rather than checking with your mind to see if what God is asking is reasonable.

CHAPTER 41

Hear and Do

James 1:22 tells us, "But be doers of the Word [obey the message], and not merely listeners to it, betraying yourselves [into deception by reasoning contrary to the Truth]."

As a Christian, for a long time I didn't understand that believers could know what God wanted them to do then deliberately say "no." I'm not talking about those who turn their backs on Jesus and want nothing to do with His salvation. I'm talking about those who disobey in the seemingly little things and don't seem to be troubled by doing so. I was one of them for many years and did not even realize the terrible impact of walking in my own will.

In verses 23 and 24, James goes on to say if we only listen to the Word, but don't obey it, it's like looking at our reflection in a mirror then going away and forgetting what we saw. But a doer of the Word, he says, is like one "who looks carefully into the faultless law, the [law] of liberty, and is faithful to it and perseveres in looking into it, being not a heedless listener who forgets but an active doer [who obeys], he shall be blessed in his doing (his life of obedience)" (v. 25). We are not blessed just because we hear the Word; we must take the next step and obey it.

Whenever Christians are faced with God's Word, and it calls them to action but they refuse to obey, their own human reasoning is often the cause. They have deceived themselves into believing something other than the truth. It's as if they think they are smarter than God. It is amazing how quickly we can talk ourselves out of doing something when deep down inside we really don't want to do it.

I've met people who seem to think God always wants them to feel good, and if something happens to make them feel bad, they don't think it could possibly be God. Or they dismiss what God is telling them simply because "it doesn't make sense."

One woman, referring to Paul's instruction to "be unceasing in prayer" (1 Thessalonians 5:17), said that verse kept coming to her every time she prayed. "What do you think that means?" I asked her.

"Oh, I think it means that day in and day out, we are to pray when we feel a need or when we want something."

Her words shocked me. "What about fellowship with the Lord?" I asked. "Isn't that a good reason? Or maybe God just wants you to spend time reading His Word and praying about what you read."

"I have too many things to do," she said. "That's fine for people who like to sit and read and pray for hours every day, but that's not the way for me."

In our brief conversation, I learned that her decisions about obeying God's Word depended on whether or not it was convenient for her lifestyle. When she read things in the Bible that didn't fit with the way she lived, she explained it to herself in such a way that she convinced herself God didn't expect her to do that.

By contrast, I remember a very dignified woman who had been a member of a traditional church most of her life. She often spoke of the noise and confusion in charismatic churches (although she had not been to one). Then she visited one of the services where I spoke and was transformed. "I couldn't believe that God would ask me to do something like clap my hands or sing loudly or even shout. But when I saw the joy on the faces of those in the congregation and heard you quote the Bible verse that says, "Oh clap your hands all you people, shout unto God with a voice of triumph" [see Psalm 47:1] what else could I do?

She said, "I had to believe God over and above what I thought or felt." She had exactly the right attitude. She didn't try to reason it out or wonder why God commanded her to take that kind of action.

> When the Bible speaks about obeying the Lord, it is not a suggestion.

She believed His Word and simply obeyed.

When the Bible speaks about obeying the Lord, it is not a suggestion. His Word doesn't ask, "Would you like to obey?" God commands us to take action by being a doer of His Word, and when we are obedient, He promises we will be blessed.

CHAPTER 42

Will You Be Critical or Helpful?

Have you ever met someone who had "the gift of suspicion"? They are everywhere—even in church. Recently I heard a man commenting about such a woman in his church. He said she always seemed to think the worst of everyone. If someone did something generous, she would say, "What does he expect to get out of that? He probably just wants everyone's gratitude."

On one occasion, an acquaintance commented about what a friendly, happy person an usher was. "That's his public face," the woman said. "He's always smiling, but I'll bet when he gets home and away from everyone else, he doesn't smile like that." He went on to ask if someone had chided her for her critical attitude; the woman only responded by saying, "I just call things as I see them. You're always trying to make things look better than they are."

The man finally realized it wasn't good for him to be around her, and he began to distance himself from her as much as possible. I believe this man made a good decision, but it was also important what he decided to do after that. Would he pray for her or begin to gossip and be critical just as she was?

I have discovered during my years in ministry that when someone with a critical spirit comes into a group or a meeting, it doesn't take much for others to become infected with it. It reminds me of the saying about one bad apple spoiling the whole bushel.

Over the years, I've met people who were very much like this lady. They're often tormented by their judgmental attitudes, critical spirits, and suspicious minds. They also destroy many relationships by their words.

Matthew 7:18–20 says these "bad fruits" tell us a lot about the "tree," but we still need to be careful we don't fall into Satan's trap by being critical of someone who is critical. Instead of judging we should pray and perhaps encourage the person who is critical to be more positive and believe the best. We must remember no one is perfect—each of us is a work in progress. Part of being a loving, caring Christian is to realize people may not see things in this life exactly as we do. We are not all at the same level of Christian maturity, but we can be sure God knows everything about each one of us. We must leave any judging to the only righteous judge—Jesus Christ. We may have times in life when it would be wise to distance ourselves from someone who consistently brings forth bad fruit, but we don't want to fall into the trap of being critical and judgmental ourselves. Prayer is always the best response to everything!

> Instead of judging we should pray and perhaps encourage the person who is critical to be more positive and believe the best.

James writes:

> [My] brethren, do not speak evil about or accuse one another. He that maligns a brother or judges his brother is maligning and criticizing the Law and judging the Law. But if you judge the Law, you are not a practicer of the Law but a censor and judge [of it]. One only is the Lawgiver and Judge Who is able to save and to destroy [the one Who has the absolute power of life

> and death]. [But you] who are you that [you presume to] pass judgment on your neighbor? (James 4:11–12).

Paul asks, "Who are you to pass judgment on and censure another's household servant? It is before his own master that he stands or falls. And he shall stand and be upheld, for the Master (the Lord) is mighty to support him and make him stand" (Romans 14:4).

CHAPTER 43

Passing Judgment

I believe pointing a finger at someone in judgment is often the way some people cover up their own weaknesses. Their theory seems to be, "Judge others before they have a chance to judge you." I remember a girl in our neighborhood who constantly pointed to obese people and said terrible things about them. She was plump herself, and I often wondered if she criticized others in an effort to keep people from noticing her weight, or perhaps to avoid dealing with her own problem.

I grew up in a family where judgment and criticism were a part of everyday life. So I became an expert at deciding how other people should live. The devil loves to keep us busy, mentally judging the faults of others. And the shortcomings in other people are often easy to see, especially when we're looking for them.

There was a time when I enjoyed sitting in the mall, observing people as they walked by. I could usually find something wrong with every one of them. I could point out bad hairstyles, out-of-style clothes, and any number of other "problems." When we choose to be judgmental, we will find there is no end to the possibilities.

Notice I used the words "choose to be judgmental," because that's exactly what I did. Had anyone called me judgmental or critical, I would have denied it, because I wasn't aware of my negative attitude. I thought I was just giving my innocent opinion. At that time, I wasn't aware my attitude was totally unloving and that I just needed to mind my own business.

Another thing I didn't think about then was the uselessness of my opinions. I didn't help anyone by pointing out to my friends what I perceived to be other people's shortcomings. I now know we can choose the thoughts on which we want to focus. We can't always choose the thoughts coming into our minds, but we can decide whether to let them stay and fester or to push them aside. Jesus said, "Do not judge and criticize and condemn others, so that you may not be judged and criticized and condemned yourselves. For just as you judge and criticize and condemn others, you will be judged and criticized and condemned, and in accordance with the measure you [use to] deal out to others, it will be dealt out again to you" (Matthew 7:1–2).

It took me a while, but I eventually learned when the devil brings those harsh, unkind, judgmental thoughts to us, we can use God's Word to chase them away.

I went through many years of misery because I judged others. It took me a long time to replace those negative thoughts with all the good things I had to think about, but the Holy Spirit kept working with me and eventually with His help I was able to overcome being critical and judgmental toward others.

During the process, God began to hold me accountable for my critical spirit, pointing me to the words of Paul:

> Why do you criticize and pass judgment on your brother?... Why do you look down upon or despise your brother? For we shall all stand before the judgment seat of God....And so each of us shall give an account of himself [give an answer in reference to judgment] to God. Then let us no more criticize and blame and pass judgment on one another, but rather decide and endeavor never to put a stumbling block or an obstacle or a hindrance in the way of a brother (Romans 14:10, 12–13).

Who are we? We're God's people. As Christians, we're part of one family—God's family. And He wants us to love and protect our family members instead of judging them. Not only is it important to stop being critical in simple obedience to God, but we should also realize that as long as we are critical we will not be happy ourselves. What we think about is what we nourish ourselves with. Another way to say it is we eat what we think and speak. Do you want to eat garbage or good, fresh, healthy food? We need to ask God to help us completely renew our minds so we learn to think with the mind of Christ and are able to do as He would.

> As long as we are critical we will not be happy ourselves.

CHAPTER 44

Loving One Another

***H**ate* is an extremely strong and harsh word. John uses that word in 1 John 2:9–11: "Whoever says he is in the Light and [yet] hates his brother [Christian, born-again child of God his Father] is in darkness even until now. Whoever loves his brother [believer] abides (lives) in the Light, and in It or in him there is no occasion for stumbling or cause for error or sin. But he who hates (detests, despises) his brother [in Christ] is in darkness and walking (living) in the dark; he is straying and does not perceive or know where he is going, because the darkness has blinded his eyes."

Any discussion among believers about *hating* other Christians would lead most of them to say, "I don't believe I have ever hated anyone." If we think about these words of John, however, perhaps he didn't mean *hate* as we think of it—feeling great hostility or animosity toward someone. Perhaps our form of hatred today is more like *indifference.* We don't really dislike people, but we don't care enough to help them when they have troubles and problems.

"Most of the loving I see today in the church is based on convenience," someone told me recently. He went on to say we will reach out to others as long as it's convenient or doesn't demand too much time or effort. This opens a wide door of opportunity for Satan to separate us from those who most need our love. Jesus commanded us to love each other. In John 13:34–35, He said people would recognize us as His disciples by our expressions of love toward one another. Perhaps one reason they don't say that about many of today's

Christians is because too often we're unwilling to go out of our way to meet the needs of others.

Love is an action verb. If you love others, you do things for them. To hate (in the biblical sense) is to do nothing or turn away. To make it worse, many people judge and criticize others and think, *If you were more obedient to God maybe you would not have the trouble you have.* We need to be compassionate, not critical.

We need to see that if we practice God's "love walk," we not only grow ourselves, but we enable others to grow. The devil can't do us much harm if we truly walk in loving relationship with others.

During my fourth pregnancy, I was extremely sick. When I prayed for healing, God reminded me I had criticized another woman in our church who was always tired and sick during her pregnancy. I said she was just weak-willed and needed to stop being such a complainer. Now, here I was in the same circumstances. I realized how wrong I was and repented. But it took more than repenting—it also became a time of learning for me. God forced me to realize how often I judged or criticized others because they didn't measure up to the standards I thought they ought to live by.

All of us make mistakes. All of us have weaknesses. God didn't call us to point out those weaknesses to the person (or worse, to someone else), but He did call us to care—to show Christ's love in any way we can. That is the way we can win over satanic attacks. Paul said not to grieve the Holy Spirit of God and to let all bitterness, wrath, anger, and evil-speaking be put away from you with all malice (see Ephesians 4:30–32).

God used these verses to help me see that being Jesus' disciple means being kind to others, tenderhearted, understanding, and forgiving. I also realized it often means overlooking their weaknesses and shortcomings. If we truly love others as Christ loves us, it isn't difficult at all.

The main thing the world is looking for is love. Most of the time they look in all the wrong places, but if they do look to the church or a Christian they should not be disillusioned and disappointed. Jesus said they should know us by our love.

Jesus was walking along and saw a fig tree in the distance covered with leaves. He was hungry so He went to the fig tree to eat some of the fruit that was supposed to be underneath the leaves. He found no fruit and cursed the tree saying it would never bear fruit again. I believe Jesus cursed the tree because it was a phony. It had leaves and no fruit. We must make sure we are not Christians with leaves and no fruit. We might have a large Christian library, good church attendance, and a bumper sticker that says, "Honk if you love Jesus." We might wear a cross necklace and even listen to Christian music, but if we are not walking in love and the other fruit of the spirit we can be a huge disappointment to someone who is truly searching for something genuine to believe in. I urge you to make walking in love a priority in your life.

If we are not walking in love and the other fruit of the spirit we can be a huge disappointment to someone who is truly searching for something genuine to believe in.

CHAPTER 45

Guarding Our Hearts

In Proverbs 4:23 we read that God tells us to guard our hearts—to watch over them carefully. But what does that really mean? It means to be alert or watchful about the ways of the enemy. It is easy to become careless about guarding our hearts and being alert to Satan's subtle tactics when things are going our way and God is pouring out His blessings on our lives. It is sad, but the truth is, when things go really well for a long time we often get lazy and stop doing what we should be doing. We need to guard our hearts diligently, not just occasionally.

Instead of using the word *guard*, I like to think of it this way: We need to post a sentinel around our hearts. Think of what a guard or sentinel does—he's on duty. He watches for the enemy to attack. He's not just ready; he's actively watchful and prepared to resist all attacks from the enemy. This is how we need to live—with a trustworthy sentinel. It doesn't mean we live in fear or constantly have to check to see if the devil is sneaking around. Think of it more as posting a sentinel to do that for us.

What kind of sentinel do we need? I think of the two most obvious ones: prayer and the Word of God. If we pray for God's Holy Spirit to help us guard our hearts, He will honor that request. When the enemy creeps up, the Holy Spirit will remind us of a scripture and we can meditate on it or speak it out loud and the enemy will flee.

In Philippians 4:6–7, Paul says not to fret or have any anxiety about anything; in a sense he is saying, if we push away our anxieties (which we do by prayer) and fill our hearts with thanksgiving,

God's peace stands guard over us. God helps us resist the attack of the enemy.

Don't minimize thanksgiving, for it is powerful. As we give thanks to God through our words and our songs, we are guarding our hearts. As the old hymn says, we should count our blessings one by one and name them to rehearse what God has done for us. It is more than just singing a few words; it is actually pausing on purpose to remember all the good things God has done in our lives. As we rejoice over past blessings, we open ourselves to more blessings in the future.

Another ally we sometimes overlook is other believers. When we're aware of our weaknesses, we can agree in prayer with other believers. We can ask them to pray specifically that we won't be misled or defeated by the enemy. Other believers can intercede for us—just as we can for them. What better guards can we post than those who cry out to God on behalf of others? The devil doesn't like hearing such prayers.

> What better guards can we post than those who cry out to God on behalf of others? The devil doesn't like hearing such prayers.

One of our responsibilities as Christians is to guard our hearts. We must be careful what we permit to come into them. Being victorious does not just automatically happen; we must be diligent to do our part. We don't receive from God by merely wishing, but we must act on His instructions to us. The enemy is always lurking around waiting for an opening into our lives, but as we follow the leading of the Holy Spirit, Satan will be continually disappointed.

CHAPTER 46

Overcoming Passivity

To be passive means to be inactive. A passive person is one who would like to see something good take place and then waits to see if it does. That desire is right, but the person takes no action. If passive people spot a need, they usually say something like, "That is just not right, someone needs to do something about it." It never occurs to them that the "someone" who needs to do something might be them. Inactivity is very dangerous. Empty space is a breeding ground for the devil. Jesus warned that if an evil spirit was cast out and the space he occupied was swept clean and kept empty the evil spirit not only would come back but would bring others with him and the last state of the man would be worse than the first.

For example, if we cast down a wrong thought we need to replace it with a positive one; otherwise the devil will simply drop another wrong one in our minds. Always remember, empty space is still a place and the Bible says we are to give no room or foothold to the devil (see Ephesians 4:27).

I once read an article about diets in which the author said most people who diet do lose weight—until they stop dieting. When they stop working at the problem, they not only stop losing, but they're worse than before they started. The author went on to say that the only way to win the battle of being overweight is to make a lifestyle change—by becoming aware of the danger areas and guarding ourselves against making wrong choices.

It works that way spiritually as well. One way to keep wrong thoughts out of your mind is to keep the mind active and alert and full of right things. You can cast out the devil, but then you must remain alert, always aware of his tricks.

There are aggressive sins (sins of commission), and there are passive sins (sins of omission). That is, there are things we do that hurt a relationship, such as speaking careless words. But we also hurt relationships by the omission of kind words, those thoughtful words that express appreciation, affection, or awareness of kind deeds done by others.

When confronted, passive individuals yell, "But I didn't do anything!" That's exactly the point. It's what they don't do. Their lack of action actually invites the devil back into their lives.

That's a strong statement, so I will say it a different way. You can win any time you take action and push away the thoughts and desires not coming from God. You may do this through prayer, reading the Bible, or even resisting the passive feelings that may be natural for you. But once you've been set free, that's only the beginning. It's not just one victory that lasts forever. It's an ongoing battle—it's being willing to constantly resist if you need to. Satan seeks to wear out God's people, but if we are persistent we will outlast him.

The best, easiest, and most effective way to resist the devil is to fill your mind and your heart with praises to God. When you worship and praise God, you've slammed the door in the enemy's face and put up a "No Trespassing" sign.

> The best, easiest, and most effective way to resist the devil is to fill your mind and your heart with praises to God.

I don't want to make it sound as if you have to fight evil every second of your life. That's a trick of the devil himself to make you feel defeated before you even get started. We do have difficult times but we also have times of great blessing. The Bible promises God won't allow more to come on us than we can bear, but with every temptation He always provides the way out (see 1 Corinthians 10:13).

CHAPTER 47

Right Action Follows Right Thinking

A friend once talked about a building bought by his church. "Function follows form," he said, as he described the shape of the building and the size of the rooms and how that determined how they could best use the building.

As I thought about it, I realized that's exactly how our lives work. Once we decide the form, the function follows. This could be stated another way: Once we set our minds to something—that's the form—the function, or the action, follows. Many people want to change their actions but not their thoughts. They want to be free from anger, gossip, lust, dishonesty, or lying. They want the bad behavior to stop, but they don't want to change their bad thinking.

The principle of God's Word is simple: Right action follows right thinking. None of us ever walks in victory unless we understand and put this principle into practice. We won't change our behavior until we change our way of thinking.

Many people struggle over trying to do the right thing. One woman told me she had been a real gossip—not that her words were always evil, but she just liked to talk. It was as if she felt compelled to be the first person to know anything and then to pass it on as quickly as possible. She struggled with holding back or saying less, and it frequently ended up causing trouble.

My advice to her was, "Until you change your way of thinking, you won't be free." Then I said I would be glad to pray for her, but added, "You must be accountable."

She interrupted me and quickly said, "I am—and I will be." I could tell she didn't really hear me so I said, "No, you haven't heard me. You want deliverance from all the gossip, but you don't want to make any changes in your thinking. It just doesn't work that way. You need deliverance in your mind; then your words and actions will change."

She resisted my words, but she did ask me to pray for her, which I did. When I finished, she began to cry. "As you prayed, I understood. God showed me that the root of my problem is how insignificant and unimportant I feel. When I'm the first to pass on information, it makes me feel good—at least for a while—and important."

She had to shift her thinking and learn to accept that she was worthwhile and loved by God just for being who she was. Once she learned to change her way of thinking—and she did over the course of weeks—she no longer had these problems with her tongue.

It's impossible to change wrong behavior to right behavior without an attitude adjustment, which means we first must change the way we think.

> It's impossible to change wrong behavior to right behavior without an attitude adjustment, which means we first must change the way we think.

I like the way Paul contrasted the old nature with the renewed mind. In Ephesians 4:22–24, he admonishes his readers: "Strip yourselves of your former nature [put off and discard your old unrenewed self] which characterized your previous manner of life.... And be constantly renewed in the spirit of your mind [having a fresh mental and spiritual attitude], and put on the new nature." Another translation puts it this way: "Let the Spirit change your way of thinking, and make you into a new person..." (vv. 23–24 CEV).

There it is: Let the Holy Spirit change your way of thinking. That's the only way you can make permanent changes in your life.

CHAPTER 48

Be Thankful—Always

Someone once told me there are more exhortations in the Bible to praise God than there are of any other kind. I don't know if that's true, but it ought to be. When our minds flow with thanksgiving and praise, we develop immunity to the devil's infectious ways.

If we complain or grumble, the opposite is true. The more we complain, the worse life gets, the more victorious the devil becomes, and the more defeated we feel. It is interesting to note as we study the history of the nation of Israel, this kind of negative attitude was the major problem causing them to wander in the wilderness for forty years before entering the Promised Land. We may call it by many names, but God called it unbelief.

God's attitude is if His people really believe Him and continue to have faith in Him, then no matter what happens in life they will know He is big enough to handle it and to make it work out for their good. Joy and peace are found in believing, not in murmuring, grumbling, finding faults, or complaining. If we are going to live in victory, praise has to be one of our major weapons. A wise pastor once told me, "Praise fills the heaven and the earth with God's presence and drives away the darkness. So if you want to live in the sunshine, praise the Lord."

When good things happen to us, most of us turn to praise. It's easy to lift our hands and our voices when God answers our prayers and delivers us from problems. It's not always easy when things go wrong or we have to wait for an answer. What do we do when we're sick or lose our jobs or people talk against us? How do we fill our minds with joyful thanksgiving in the midst of those situations?

Two verses give us options. First Thessalonians 5:18 tells us, "Thank [God] in everything [no matter what the circumstances may be, be thankful and give thanks], for this is the will of God for you [who are] in Christ Jesus [the Revealer and Mediator of that will]," and Philippians 4:4 says, "Rejoice in the Lord always [delight, gladden yourselves in Him]; again I say, Rejoice!"

The negative option is to take the attitude of Job's wife, who was so shaken up by the loss of her children and their possessions that she cried out, "Do you still hold fast your blameless uprightness? Renounce God and die!" (Job 2:9).

Job answered with great wisdom: "You speak as one of the impious and foolish women would speak. What? Shall we accept [only] good at the hand of God and shall we not accept [also] misfortune and what is of a bad nature?" (v. 10). Job understood a righteous life doesn't mean everything always runs smoothly and only blessings fall on top of blessings.

We have two positive options open to us. Most of us can practice the first, but not all of us can accept the second. The first is to praise God *in spite of* what's going on in our lives. Or another way to say that is in the midst of our troubles and hardships, we can choose to look for things that are not wrong and rejoice over them. It may take effort, but if we can turn our eyes away from the immediate problems, we can see that everything in life isn't bad. We can also rejoice because God has faithfully taken us through the turmoil of the past, and we can rejoice and know He will do the same thing again.

The second option when circumstances are difficult is to ask, "God, what can I learn from this? What do You want to teach me through this so I can be closer to You and rejoice more fully in Your goodness?" That's not an easy question, and the answers are often even harder. God is not the Author of our troubles, but He may well use them to help us become better people.

God is not the Author of our troubles, but He may well use them to help us become better people.

Sometimes we only grasp the important lessons in our lives when we fall flat on our faces. The psalmist says: "Before I was afflicted I went astray, but now Your word do I keep [hearing, receiving, loving, and obeying it]" (Psalm 119:67). It isn't that God is out to hurt us, but God loves us enough to stop us and hopefully wake us up to how wrong we are living. I often think of the young man we call the Prodigal Son in the Bible. He wanted to have his inheritance early but then wasted the entire thing. He ended up with a job feeding hogs and had to eat their food. It wasn't long before he came to his senses and realized he needed to go home to his father and beg for forgiveness. His trouble finally caused him to realize the error of his ways.

Throughout my many years in ministry, I've heard stories from people who had wonderful jobs or great ministries or made a great deal of money—and then their lives fell apart. They were people who had things but not God. One man—someone who was once a millionaire—came to our meetings after he spent three years in prison. The first words out of his mouth were, "I'm glad I was convicted and sent to prison. I had run from God for a long time. The Lord finally got my attention when someone gave me a copy of Joyce Meyer's book *Healing the Brokenhearted* while I was in prison."

Not everyone can rejoice and give thanks for their suffering, but we can all give thanks in the midst of it. God has our well-being in mind and we can trust that whatever happens in life He will work out for good if we continue loving and serving Him (see Romans 8:28).

CHAPTER 49

Tips for Being Thankful

All of us know we need to be thankful. God tells us to do so, and we also know from our own experience that once we seriously start praising God, our burdens and our troubles seem to weigh less heavily on our shoulders.

That is part of the power of being thankful. As we pause to give thanks to God for what is good in our lives, we also appreciate what we have. I believe God wants us to be grateful people—people who are filled with gratitude not only toward God but also toward other people. That's my first tip: when someone does anything nice for you, let that person know you appreciate it.

> God wants us to be grateful people—people who are filled with gratitude not only toward God but also toward other people.

One day I was going into an office building, and a man standing nearby opened the door for me. I thanked him and smiled. "You're the fifth person I've held the door for," he said, "and you're the first one to smile and the second to thank me."

I thanked him a second time. Afterward, I thought how much we take others for granted, even when they do such simple things as open a door for a stranger.

Instead of accepting that as the way things are, we can develop a thankful mind. Did your bus arrive on time today? If so, did you thank the driver? When you ate at the restaurant, did you thank the server for filling your coffee cup a second time without being asked?

I could go on and on, but the point I want to make is: develop an attitude of gratitude toward the people in your life.

Here's another tip: appreciate your family members, especially the person to whom you're married. Even though Dave and I have been married a long time, I still tell him I appreciate him. He's patient with me and thoughtful. Just those few words of thanks are a great way to develop a thankful mind and heart. Showing appreciation is one of the best ways to improve relationships.

When you express appreciation, it's good for the other person to hear the words, but also remember it releases joy in you. You enrich both your life and another person's life, even by appreciating small things.

Another thing you can do is meditate daily on things for which you can be thankful. I heard of one man who won't get out of bed in the morning until he has thanked God for at least ten things. He counts them on his fingers, and they're small things really, such as having a reliable car to drive, being a member of an exciting Sunday school class, or just being thankful he's healthy. I often thank God for having hot water. I really enjoy taking a hot bath and I am aware that multitudes of people in the world don't even have clean water to drink, let alone the simple joy of sitting in a bathtub filled with hot water.

The man I mentioned also has the habit prior to going to sleep of focusing on at least three things that went well that day. He relives those three positive things. For him, it can be as simple as his supervisor telling him what a good job he did on a project or an affirming e-mail from a friend.

Here's another tip: Be thankful for the honesty in other people. No one likes to hear negative things, but sometimes you need to hear them. Of course, they may momentarily hurt your feelings, but you still can learn and grow from the experience.

I have a friend who says, "Only two people will tell you the truth about yourself: someone who's angry at you and someone who loves you very much." God uses both types of people in our lives.

So be thankful for people who tell you the truth about yourself, even if it's not what you want to hear. When you hear the truth—especially something of which you're not aware, you can change. And after you've changed, isn't that just one more thing for which you can be thankful?

The things to be thankful for are really too many to count, but sadly we miss many of them simply because we don't purposely look for them. This is a good time to decide to form a new habit of being extremely thankful and saying so.

CHAPTER 50

Jesus Came to Set You Free

The Bible says Jesus came to open prison doors, open blinded eyes, and set the captives free (see Isaiah 61:1). When it speaks of blind eyes it is not only speaking of those physically blind. Jesus did heal those who had no natural sight, but He also wants to open our eyes to what He has provided for us, that which we may be missing through lack of knowledge. I attended church regularly for many years without ever hearing Jesus wanted to set me free from my past and other things that kept me in a prison of defeat and discouragement. I heard Jesus died for my sins and because of Him I could be forgiven and have the hope of heaven, but I did not hear anything that was helping me live my daily life in victory.

What kind of bondages do you have in your life? Are you frustrated, confused, unhappy, or discontent with yourself and your life? Do you experience guilt, condemnation, fear or worry, and anxiety? If so, you need to hear the good news that Jesus came to help you realize those prison doors have been opened by Him and you are free to walk out and begin a new life lived with and for Him.

It is good to look forward to heaven, but what about right now? Are you enjoying your life now? If not, you need to know it is God's will for you to do so. Jesus said He came that we might have and enjoy life abundantly (see John 10:10).

I want to encourage you to make a decision that you will have and enjoy everything Jesus died to give you. Press past the things holding you in bondage to the glorious life of freedom available to you right now.

I lived for many years as a Christian still held in bondage to the pain of my past. I had a bitter attitude, self-pity, resentment, and many other negative emotions. These things were actually my prison. We do not have to be in a physical prison to be in prison. Mental and emotional prisons may indeed be worse than a physical one. People may be free to move about and go here and there, but if they are continually tormented in their souls they are not truly free.

> Mental and emotional prisons may indeed be worse than a physical one. A person may be free to move about and go here and there, but if they are continually tormented in their soul they are not truly free.

As I studied God's Word and began to learn that Jesus came to set me free from all those tormenting things, and that my past had no power over my future, I truly began to enjoy each day of my life.

Emotional and mental freedom may be a new thought for you. Perhaps you have passively put up with a tormented soul, but I am announcing to you that Jesus died to set you completely free. He has opened all your prison doors, and as soon as you realize it you will be able to take His hand and walk out into a new and glorious life.

I suggest you begin praying about each tormenting emotion or mental habit you have and find scripture about those areas. For example, if you are prone to worrying all the time, pray specifically about freedom in that area and look for all the scripture you can find about worry and anxiety. Study what God's Word says about peace and refuse to live without it. It is yours, bought and paid for with the blood of Jesus, so why not claim it and start a new life today.

The apostle Paul said in Philippians 3:12 that he was determined to take hold of those things for which Christ Jesus died. In other words he made a decision that he would learn to have and enjoy everything Jesus died to give him. He mentioned pressing past things and that is exactly what we must be willing to do. It takes no effort at all to remain in bondage, but effort is required to gain and maintain freedom. Claiming your rights as a believer in Jesus will take some diligence and determination on your part. You will have to study, pray, and refuse to remain in bondage, but there is a life of freedom waiting for you that is more wonderful than you can imagine. Make a decision today that Jesus died to set you free and free you will be!!!

CHAPTER 51

Do You Need a Change of Address?

I find it difficult to believe what the people of Israel said in Numbers 20:2–4: "Now there was no water for the congregation, and they assembled together against Moses and Aaron. And the people contended with Moses, and said, Would that we had died when our brethren died [in the plague] before the Lord! And why have you brought up the congregation of the Lord into this wilderness, that we should die here, we and our livestock?"

How could they have said such a terrible thing? "Would that we had died when our brethren died [in the plague] before the Lord!" Were they actually saying they would rather suffer, be in torment, and die in slavery than to live free and with God?

It is difficult to believe anyone would choose one or the other over freedom but the truth is people do it all the time. God was offering the Israelites a new life, but they continually murmured and complained about every inconvenience they encountered. They wanted to behave however they felt like behaving, yet they expected good results. The sooner we realize that never works, the better off we will be. God's promises are available for all. But they are not available unless we are willing to do things God's way.

We cannot do bad things and expect good results. We cannot grumble at God and expect divine blessings. That is what the Israelites did. They were impatient, they murmured continually, they felt sorry for themselves, they were not thankful, and they blamed Moses and even God when things went wrong. They had an opportunity to press through to the Promised Land, yet they died in the wilderness. How can that be? How can they be so confused and twisted in their thinking? But then, I was the same way for many years and I know people like that today.

Jane married an alcoholic named John, and when he went into his drunken rages, he beat her. She left, took their children, and divorced him. Two years later, Jane married again. She married John again—oh, not *that* John. The second husband's name was Ralph. He was a drunkard, and she repeated the same sad and abusive story. Her third *John* was named Ken. Although their names were different, it was as if she married the same man (the same kind of man) three times.

When I met Jane, she grumbled and asked, "Are there any good men out there?" Of course, she later admitted she looked for men in all the wrong places. She usually found them at a bar or a party she should not have attended. She didn't go to church or any kind of Bible studies. She never put herself in a place to even meet a decent man, but she continually complained. The truth is she was making bad choices and then having a "poor me" attitude about the results. It is foolish to think we can see change if we keep doing the same things over and over.

If you desire change in your life, you will have to make some different choices than the ones you have made in the past. Do you need a change of address? Are you tired of wilderness living and prefer to live in the Promised Land, a place where many good things abound? If that is what you truly want, you can have it, but you will have to be willing to change many things in your life.

It is easy to condemn the Israelites because the Bible lays out their story so clearly. Paul wrote about the wilderness wanderings and urged his readers to not "discontentedly complain as some of them did—and were put out of the way entirely by the destroyer (death)" (1 Corinthians 10:10–11). As long as you continue to act as the Israelites did in their grumbling, you will get the same results. As long as you live like Jane, you will have the same disastrous effects. Although I gave the example of Jane, these situations abound in many people's lives. Perhaps you are someone who has your paycheck spent before you cash it. Or maybe you are easily offended and end up angry most of the time. Regardless of your situation, as long as you continue with bad choices, you will end up with bad outcomes.

As long as you continue with bad choices, you will end up with bad outcomes.

When you are really tired of getting the same negative results—when you are tired of Satan buffeting you and tormenting you—you are ready to make changes. Those people in the wilderness died outside the Promised Land because they never learned. You have an advantage: you know about them, and you also know the Holy Spirit wants to change you.

You *can* change. You can begin by asking God to help you think positive thoughts in line with His positive thoughts, because positive thinking produces positive attitudes. Once your attitude changes, your life changes. It requires some effort and persistence, but it is definitely worth it. It is really quite simple: make the decision that God is smarter than you and start doing things His way.

CHAPTER 52

Instant Gratification

"Instant gratification takes too long," my friend said, laughing. She was standing in front of the microwave. She set the timer for ninety seconds to heat her coffee and tapped her toe as she impatiently waited.

I smiled as I watched, but then I realized that we've been spoiled by the word *instant* in our lives today. We have instant credit approval, instant oatmeal, instant coffee and drive-through everything. We like to think God's ways are the same, but they are not. "God, give it to me now," we pray. Or if we don't use those words, that's what we mean.

One of the things I've learned from my years of Bible study is we can't hurry the Lord. He does things in His time. The Bible tells us about the long waits of Abraham and Joseph before God fulfilled His promises to them. Moses fled into the wilderness after killing a man, and waited forty years for God to tap him on the shoulder. Rachel prayed for years to have a child, and so did Hannah, before God answered them.

> We can't hurry the Lord. He does things in His time.

We should learn from the countless examples in the Bible of people required to be patient that we cannot hurry God. Many people grow impatient in waiting, and of course, the devil uses that to sneer and say, "God isn't going to do what He promised. If He were going to do it, He would have done it by now."

As I've thought about the matter of human impatience, I've realized that impatience is the fruit of pride. The proud can't seem to wait for anything with a proper attitude. It's as if they cry out, "I deserve it—and I deserve it *right now*."

I want to point out something from the words of James 5:7. God doesn't say, "Be patient *if* you wait," but, "Be patient *as* you wait." He uses the beautiful example of farmers. They prepare the soil and plant the crops, and then comes the season of waiting. They know in God's time, the crops will produce, and they also realize it's a different growing season for tomatoes than it is for wheat. They know waiting is necessary for harvest, so instead of making themselves miserable while they wait, they enjoy the time in between seed planting and harvest. You can make a decision to do the same thing.

We need to enjoy our lives now—right now while we wait. So many people complain about wasting time (which is how they talk about waiting). Instead of pacing and grumbling about how long we have to wait in line at the grocery store or the traffic congestion on the expressway, what if we said, "Thanks, God. I can slow down now. I can enjoy this moment. Every second of my life doesn't have to be busy, busy, busy"?

The psalmist said it this way: "My times are in Your hands; deliver me from the hands of my foes and those who pursue me and persecute me" (Psalm 31:15). This was the prayer by a man in a desperate situation. His enemies were out to kill him. Still, he didn't panic, but said, "My times are in Your hands."

Isn't that how God wants you to live? Your life and your times are in God's hands. Doesn't it follow then, if you're facing delays and have to wait, God knows? He's the One Who controls the clock of life. "My times are in Your hands." That's the way God wants us to live—and to enjoy the waiting time. Don't focus just on reaching your desired destination. Focus on the journey and be determined to relish the moments God gives you to relax, and enjoy them as a gift from God Himself.

CHAPTER 53

Too Hard?

"Please make everything easy and simple for me, dear God. I don't like to struggle, and I want constant victory without exerting any effort. Let me go on my way as I let You do everything to keep me secure."

I have never heard anyone pray those words, but I have heard people ask for an easy life in prayer. Too many people want victory without battle, triumph without effort, and ease without labor. God's world simply doesn't function that way. After thirty-three years of ministry I have never had a person ask me to pray they would be able to endure their difficulty with a good attitude. They always want their problems to go away; and looking at it naturally, that makes sense. We all probably feel that way until we learn that some of our greatest blessings come out of our challenging times in life.

> Too many people want victory without battle, triumph without effort, and ease without labor. God's world simply doesn't function that way.

"It's just too hard." I wonder how many times I have heard people say that. I wonder how many times Joyce Meyer has said that. *And I have.* There was a time when I tried to make a firm stand for following the Lord, but in my heart (and often in my mouth) were the words, "It was just so hard."

God convicted me of negative thinking. He taught me that if I would stop looking at the hardships and obey Him, He would make a way for me. Deuteronomy 30:9–11, 14 tells us God wants to bless us and prosper from the work of our hands, but we must obey His commandments, and in verse 11, He assures us we can do it: "For this commandment which I command you this day is not too difficult for you, nor is it far off." The first time I saw that scripture it destroyed my lifelong excuse that what God was asking me to do was just too hard. Anytime God asks us to do something, He always gives us the ability to do it.

Because we spend so much time listening to the negatives and figuring out what can go wrong, often we forget the promise that His will is not too difficult for us. Instead, it may help if we expect our difficulties to actually work out for good. For instance, take encouragement from Joseph. After he spent years in Egypt and saved the lives of his family in Canaan, his brothers were afraid of him. Before that, they hated him, plotted to kill him, and sold him into slavery. After their father, Jacob, died, they expected Joseph to punish them. He could have done that and groaned about his hard life—and his life had not been easy. Not only was he sold as a slave by his brothers, but he was wrongly imprisoned and could have been put to death if God hadn't been with him.

Instead of saying, "Life is so hard," Joseph said, "As for you, you thought evil against me, but God meant it for good, to bring about that many people should be kept alive, as they are this day" (Genesis 50:20). He understood how God works in human lives.

Joseph didn't look only at the hardships; he looked at the opportunities. Joseph didn't listen to the whispering campaign of his enemy; he turned his ears to the encouraging words of his God. In no place do we read of him complaining. He saw everything that happened to him as something that would work out for good in the end.

Even in difficulty we need to remember God loves us and has a good plan for our lives. The devil likes to creep in to say, "If God loves you so much, why are you in this mess?"

The best answer I can give is to repeat the words of Paul the great apostle:

> Let us exult and triumph in our troubles and rejoice in our sufferings, knowing that pressure and affliction and hardship produce patient and unswerving endurance. And endurance (fortitude) develops maturity of character (approved faith and tried integrity). And character [of this sort] produces [the habit of] joyful and confident hope of eternal salvation. Such hope never disappoints or deludes or shames us, for God's love has been poured out in our hearts through the Holy Spirit Who has been given to us (Romans 5:3–5).

God never promised us a life lived on easy street, but He does promise a blessed life.

CHAPTER 54

Choosing the Right Response

When you and I begin to break ourselves of any bad habit, we have a struggle on our hands. We have to fight within ourselves, crying out to God, "Lord, help me, help me!" It is so wonderful to know that the Holy Spirit is always with us to help us all the time.

If you know you have given yourself over to some bad habit like emotional eating, when you sit down to the table you have to say within yourself, *Holy Spirit, help me not to overeat.* In a restaurant where everybody at your table is ordering dessert, and you can feel yourself starting to waiver, you can cry out inside, *Holy Spirit, help me, help me!*

I have found that if I depend upon my flesh through sheer willpower or determination alone, I will fail every time. But if I am determined to resist temptation by calling on the power of the Holy Spirit, I find the strength I need for success.

I have discovered that the Lord is not going to do everything for us in this life. We can't just find someone to pray for us to be set free from all our bondage. There is a part we must play with our minds and wills. It takes a combination of faith and action.

The apostle Paul said he did not take the grace of God in vain (see Galatians 2:21). He meant that he did not expect God to do everything for him without doing his part too. God gives us the ability to do what we need to do, but we must choose right action. We must keep our eyes on the Word of God and do what it says—not what the enemy causes us to feel like doing.

If you are going to be a person committed to the Word of God, you

> If you are going to be a person committed to the Word of God, you will have to learn to be led by the Spirit and not by your emotions.

will have to learn to be led by the Spirit and not by your emotions. Whenever an emotion rises inside me, I test it to see if it is in line with the Word of God. If it is not, the Holy Spirit reveals it to me, and I resist it.

That's how we fight against rash reactions—by using our will to make a decision to follow God's Word rather than our feelings. We have spent a lifetime reacting to most things without considering God's Word, so the change will take time. But don't be discouraged and don't ever give up!

CHAPTER 55

Developing a Compassionate Heart

Many times when people have been hurt badly in their past, they develop a hard-core attitude and build invisible walls to protect themselves. They may have all the same feelings others have, but they are unable to show them. Sometimes they may even be so hurt they become callous and unable to feel anything. In either case, there is a real need for healing.

The Lord called my attention to two things in a passage in Ephesians 4 about unbelievers. First of all, it says unbelievers are so callous and hard they are past feeling. But in the same verse it says they live by their feelings in sensuality and carnality. As I meditated on that statement, the Lord showed me that such people are past doing what they should be doing with their feelings.

God gives us feelings for a specific purpose in our walk with Him. Unbelievers have been hardened to the place they are, past using their feelings for the right purpose. Satan has moved them into an area in which they are living riotous lives, doing whatever they feel like doing. You and I are not to live by the philosophy of today's world: "If it feels good, do it!"

Jesus experienced every emotion and suffered every feeling you and I do, yet without sinning (see Hebrews 4:15). Why did He not sin? He did not give in to His wrong feelings. He knew the Word of God in every area of life because He spent years studying it before He began His ministry. The Bible says that as a child Jesus "grew and became strong in spirit, filled with wisdom" (Luke 2:40). By the time He was twelve years old, He thought He was old enough to go to the temple in Jerusalem and "be about His Father's business" (Luke 2:41–52) but He still had years of learning before He entered His full-time ministry. You and I will never be able to say no to our feelings if we don't have a strong knowledge of the Word of God within us. Jesus had the same feelings we do, but He never sinned by giving in to the bad ones.

When I am hurt by someone and I feel angry or upset, it is such a comfort to me to be able to lift my hurt to the Lord, saying, "Jesus, I am so glad You understand what I am feeling right now, and You don't condemn me for feeling this way. I don't want to give vent to my emotions. Help me, Lord, to get over them. Help me forgive those who have wronged me and not slight them, avoid them, or seek to pay them back for the harm they have done me. Help me to not live under condemnation in thinking I shouldn't be feeling this way."

It is not a matter of just thinking, *I shouldn't be feeling this way*; it is a matter of crying out to God and functioning in the fruit of the Spirit already inside us called self-control (see Galatians 5:23). You and I don't have to feel condemned because we have bad feelings. Jesus understands. His main concern is that we come to the point where we are like Him: humble, gentle, meek, and lowly. This does not mean we become a doormat for people to walk all over, but God wants us to develop compassion, understanding, and softness of heart.

Because I was hurt really badly in my childhood, I developed a hard core and built walls for self-protection, just like those I have mentioned. I became hard and calloused on the inside. But I learned and am still learning that we can become like Jesus, Who is humble, gentle, meek, and lowly, and not harsh, hard, sharp, and pressing (see Matthew 11:29–30).

No matter what our past experiences or our present feelings, we are to be compassionate toward others. We are to rejoice with those who rejoice, but we are also to weep with those who weep (see Romans 12:15).

When God gave Solomon the opportunity to ask for anything he wanted, he requested an understanding heart. No matter what anybody does or has done to us, we should pray for them and try to understand what happened to them to make them the way they are. Hurting people hurt people, but love can heal and change them. Anybody can be tough, harsh, and hard-hearted, but those who seek God can be tender, compassionate, and understanding.

It is obvious Satan wants us to develop hardness and callousness so we *cannot* feel or be sensitive to the needs of others. God wants us to be more sensitive to the feelings and needs of others and less sensitive to our own feelings and needs. He wants us to deposit ourselves in His hands and let Him take care of us while we are practicing being kind and compassionate and sensitive to other people. As believers, we are not to be led by our negative feelings, but we are to be moved by compassion and understanding to those in need. This can only happen when we bend our will to God's will.

As believers, we are not to be led by our negative feelings, but we are to be moved by compassion and understanding to those in need.

CHAPTER 56

Proper Timing

I would like to give you an assignment. I'm suggesting that you read the book of Proverbs and notice how often it speaks of wisdom. It never tells us to be led by emotion, but it strongly encourages us to pursue wisdom. I like to say wisdom does now what it will be satisfied with later. It does not merely do what it feels like doing, but it chooses what is right.

I think we all know that people led by their feelings do not want to wait for anything. They want everything right now, but as you study Proverbs one of the things you will learn is wisdom waits for the proper time to do things.

> Wisdom always waits for the right time to act.

Wisdom always waits for the right time to act, while our personal desires call for immediate action. Emotionalism is rash. It does not stop to consider the outcome of its actions. While wisdom calmly looks ahead to determine how a decision will affect the future, feelings are only concerned with what is happening at the moment. "Be not rash with your mouth, and let not your heart be hasty to utter a word before God" (Ecclesiastes 5:2).

How many times have you said or done something in the heat of the moment, then later experienced deep, deep regret for your rash action? "Oh, if I had only kept my mouth shut!" It is amazing the damage that can be done to a relationship by one emotional outburst.

One time, when I was trying to learn to control my mouth and not talk back to my husband, I got so emotional the Lord had to say to me, "Joyce, that's enough! Don't you say another word!" I hurriedly left the room, ran down the hall, and locked myself in the bathroom. I was so upset I buried my face in a towel and screamed into it! Sometimes the strongholds in our flesh become so ingrained it takes some pretty determined action to break them down. That's why we need to learn to fight against our undisciplined desires and bring them into submission to the will of God.

How many times would things have turned out quite differently in your life had you only waited and seriously thought about a decision before you made it? We can all think of many times like that, so let's at least learn from our mistakes and not keep doing the same destructive thing over and over. We think it is hard to wait and often say that, but the really hard thing is behaving rashly and then spending days, months, or even years trying to undo the damage done in that moment of reaction.

Even when I am making a serious purchase I often walk away from the item for five or ten minutes, giving my emotions an opportunity to subside before I decide what I want to do. Most of the world is in deep debt because of emotional spending. Something they see gets them excited, and their desire hinders common sense and reason. I really encourage you to make a decision to be an expert at waiting for proper timing. Don't do things you don't have peace in your heart about doing.

Thousands of people struggle trying to keep commitments they made in a time of heated emotion. Think before you make a promise and make sure you really want to do long term what is going to be required.

Your Emotions

CHAPTER 57

God Gave Us Emotions to Enjoy Life

At times we enjoy our emotions and the support they give us. At other times, when our emotions work against us, we would rather be rid of them! It is important to recognize that God gave us emotions for a reason. Our job is not to try to rid ourselves of emotions but learn how to manage them.

Our job is not to try to rid ourselves of emotions but learn how to manage them.

For example, God caused me to understand anger is just an emotion He gave us for a reason like the other emotions He gave us. Like pain, anger warns us something is wrong. Without the capacity to become angry, we wouldn't recognize mistreatment of ourselves or another. The Bible does not teach that we are never to feel anger. Instead it teaches us when we do become angry, we are not to sin, but rather we are to manage or control our anger in the proper way: "Be ye angry, and sin not: let not the sun go down upon your wrath" (Ephesians 4:26 KJV).

There was a time when God gave me a revelation about the truth of that scripture. One day as I was about to leave home to go preach, I became angry with my husband. Guilt and condemnation came over me. I thought, *Joyce, how can you go out and preach to others after getting angry like that this morning?* Of course, I was still angry and the question really bothered me. As I began to meditate on it, the Lord revealed to me the truth of the above verse in Ephesians which says to be angry and sin not. He let me know that feeling anger is not a sin, but acting on it improperly or not being willing to let it go is sin.

Problems with anger, as with our other emotions, come when Satan tries to use and abuse our anger to lead us into sin. Many times people come to me for counseling, saying, "I have this deep-seated anger inside me." This type of anger is often a wound left over from childhood hurts. In that case, the answer is not merely to get rid of the anger, but to get at the root of what caused it in the first place.

It is not right to go around feeling angry all the time, any more than it is right to go around feeling pain all the time. Many Christians have the false idea they are never to become angry. When they become angry, they condemn themselves for even feeling angry. No matter how hard we try, we will always have to deal with the emotion of anger.

Many people who struggle with controlling the anger they feel rising are surprised to hear it is actually possible to learn how to control their emotions. We need to learn how to start dealing with them instead of simply venting or repressing and consequently feeling guilty and condemned because of them. Here is another example you might relate to. Imagine for a moment that you are looking through a magazine or a catalog and you spot a photograph of an attractive person of the opposite sex. Suddenly you feel a sexual emotion. Does this mean you are perverted and have something desperately wrong with you? Does it mean you are not really saved—that you don't truly love God or your spouse? No, it simply means you are human and subject to all the same emotional feelings and reactions experienced by other human beings. The important thing is how you handle your emotions. Do you keep staring at the photo or do you turn away realizing those feelings should be reserved for your marriage partner only? We all have those feelings but we are to learn, with God's help, to keep them focused toward our spouses.

Romans 6:2 tells us that if we are Christians we have died to sin. It does not tell us sin is dead! Sin still initially presents itself in the form of temptation and then it becomes a full-blown problem if we give in to the temptation. I recommend reading the sixth chapter of Romans in its entirety. If you do that, you will see that our instruction is to resist sin in the power of the Holy Spirit. We are not told we will never feel emotions, but we are told to not continue offering our bodies as instruments of sin.

It is important to remember that emotions won't disappear. They will always be there. We must not deny their existence or feel guilty because of them. Instead we are to channel them in the right direction. We are to deny the flesh the right to rule us, but we are not to deny that it exists.

The message is simple: There is nothing wrong with emotions, as long as they are kept under control. There is a way to manage our destructive emotions so we can use the good emotions in the way God intends—for example, to move in love and compassion toward others and to experience great joy in serving God.

CHAPTER 58

Negative Emotions Steal Your Energy

Do you have any idea how valuable you are? If you suffer from self-doubt or self-hatred, if you abuse your body with bad food or bad habits, even if you simply put yourself at the very bottom of the list of people you do things for, under the kids and spouse and parents and boss and friends, then you do *not* understand your own value. If you did, you wouldn't treat yourself that way. You were put on this earth to spread God's love, and nothing could be more valuable than that.

> You were put on this earth to spread God's love, and nothing could be more valuable than that.

Maybe you never learned your own importance. That's what happened to me. As a child, I was abused and taught that I was the least valuable person on the planet. It took me many years of studying God's Word and fellowshipping with Him before I got even an inkling of my own worth.

Or maybe you did know your value when you were younger, but somewhere along the way you forgot it, buried it under a to-do list that clamored louder for your attention than your own soul. If so, then join the club. The degraded value systems in the modern world pummel us with the message that our spirit, soul, and body come last, after money and food and status and stuff. No matter how hard we resist, we all succumb now and then.

I can't tell you strongly enough how important it is to reform your value system, to go back to a much older value system—*God's* value system. It applies to all people, and it puts your entire being (body, mind, will, emotions, and spirit) right at the top of God's list of important and valuable things. Your entire being plays an important role in God's plan; He's entrusted you with the great responsibility of taking care of it. Only by keeping your spirit, soul, and body in tip-top condition can you truly do God's work.

It is important to deal with negative emotions because they steal your energy and can even be the root cause of serious disease. Remember that dis-ease causes disease.

Let me give you an example. One day I was experiencing a lot of guilt over something I did wrong. Although I asked God to forgive me and actually believed He had, I still felt guilty. My mind was on my past when it should have been on my future. I felt depressed and discouraged. I had a headache, and in general did not feel like doing much of anything. The Holy Spirit began to deal with my attitude. He asked me if I thought my attitude was helping me or His work. He then said, "I want you to get over this because you are no good to Me in this condition." The Holy Spirit's straightforward way of dealing with me caused me to see that I was wasting my day on negative emotions. I was actually allowing my soul (mind, will, and emotions) to adversely affect my spirit and my body. My spirit felt oppressed and my body ached. We must realize we are complex creatures and every part of us affects the other parts.

CHAPTER 59

You Can Control Your Emotions

I used to wonder, "What is wrong with me, anyway?" Have you ever felt that way? You lie in bed in the morning, making all sorts of wonderful plans about how good you're going to be that day, but as soon as you are up, you ruin your plans. You deal with a few people, somebody does one little thing you don't like, and you turn into a totally different human being. I always say I never had any problem getting along with everybody when nobody was home. It was when they came home at night that I had a problem!

I could be so spiritual during the day, singing praises to the Lord, "I surrender all..." Then my children would maybe drop or spill something, causing me to fly into a rage—a spiritual Dr. Jekyll and Mr. Hyde. Afterward, I spent the rest of the evening under self-condemnation. The same devil who tempts you to act stupid is the same devil who comes around and condemns you for doing what he told you to do.

Some people say, "Well, I just can't help it. I lose control." Yes, we can help it. I know we can because we are able to control ourselves around particular people—people we want to impress. I could have been in the middle of the biggest fit in the whole world, but if somebody like my pastor walked up, I straightened up extremely fast and became kind and loving. We're often like different creatures when we think nobody is looking. But what really goes on in your private life shows in your public life, whether or not you know it. God is called all-seeing and all-knowing, and we're definitely not putting anything over on Him. Remember God is watching you all the time.

We need to stop thinking we can't control our emotions and start learning how to deal with and manage them in a godly way.

Excuses are just reasons stuffed with a lie. We make excuses and thereby deceive ourselves. What we are doing would be wrong for someone else, but we have an excuse for doing it. Are you ready to get rid of your "excuse bag"? I think we all have one and it is stuffed with a variety of excuses for every conceivable situation. If we are grouchy, our excuse is we feel bad or had a tough day at work. If we are selfish, we tell ourselves that if we don't take care of ourselves then nobody will. If we are spending more money than we make, we tell ourselves how wise it is to get the item while it is on sale. I encourage you to ask God to make you aware of all the excuses you make and start taking responsibility for your actions rather than excusing them.

We need to stop thinking we can't control our emotions and start learning how to deal with and manage them in a godly way.

CHAPTER 60

The Test of Emotionally Trying Times

A few years ago, as I was praying, God revealed to me, "Joyce, I am going to test your emotions." I had never heard of anything like that. Psalm 7:9 says God establishes the righteous, those upright and in harmony with Him, for Him; He tries the hearts, emotions, and thinking powers. The meaning of "tries" here means purifies. I didn't know scriptures about God trying our emotions were even in the Bible.

About six months later I suddenly seemed to become an emotional wreck. I cried for no reason. Everything hurt my feelings. I thought, *What is the problem here? What's going on?* Then the Lord reminded me of what He showed me earlier: "I am going to test your emotions." He led me to Psalm 7:9 and Revelation 2:23 and caused me to understand what He was doing was for my good.

No matter who you are, there will be periods of time in which you feel more emotional than usual. You may wake up one morning and feel like breaking down and crying for no reason. That may last a day or a week, or it may last longer. You may think, *What is my problem?*

During those times you have to be careful, because your feelings will get hurt very easily. The slightest thing will set you off. There were times in my life when I would go to bed praying, feeling as sweet as could be, then wake up the next morning like I had stayed up all night eating nails! I would get up in such a foul mood that if anyone came near me or crossed me, I felt like hitting them on the head!

What should we do when we start feeling that way? First of all, we shouldn't allow ourselves to fall under condemnation. Secondly, we shouldn't get confused trying to figure out what is happening. What we should do is simply say, "This is one of those times when my emotions are being tried and with God's help I am going to be stable. We cannot always control how we feel, but we are in control of our decisions. Part of growing up in God is learning how to hold steady in the storms of life.

> We cannot always control how we feel, but we are in control of our decisions.

Several years ago my husband and I purchased a fifty-two-year-old house and began remodeling it. Shortly after we began that project I felt in my heart God wanted me to start praying about learning to be more patient. We cannot learn patience without something to be patient about, and it seemed almost everything with the house started going wrong and there was nothing anyone could do to rush the process.

The remodeling turned into a bigger project than we thought it would be, and we needed to move in, but couldn't. I became really angry and acted in a way that did not reflect my teachings on emotions! The Bible says in Psalm 94:12–13 that blessed is the man whom God disciplines until he learns to keep himself calm in adversity.

Sometimes God allows us to go through some trying times so we will have the opportunity to learn how to control our emotions. The Bible says God will never allow any more to come upon us than we are able to bear (see 1 Corinthians 10:13). God will test our emotions and help us learn stability because it's only when we're stable that we can truly enjoy life and be a good example to other people.

CHAPTER 61

Be Mentally Prepared

I have often heard that after a person goes through a real emotional high, he will usually bottom out with an emotional low. We see this in the life of Elijah the prophet in the book of 1 Kings. One day he was on Mt. Carmel making a fool of the priests of Baal, calling down fire from heaven, at the height of his elation. The next day he was out in the desert sitting under a juniper tree asking God to let him die because he felt so depressed.

I have noticed when I minister in a series of meetings, I spend everything I have spiritually, emotionally, and mentally. I get so excited when I see what God is doing to help and minister to people and change their lives through those meetings, through my radio and television broadcasts, and through other outreaches in which we are involved.

But then when I return from something exciting like that to normal, everyday life, I have to exercise discipline not to be dissatisfied with ordinary life. Who wants to go from seeing God perform miracles one day to doing normal household chores the next?

Sometimes we think, *Oh, if I could just stay on this emotional high forever then life would be great.* But the truth is if we were constantly doing something emotionally exciting, it would not be long before we wouldn't appreciate those times. We need to be able to experience and be content with both sides of life. If we are only content during exciting times, it is our circumstances making us joyful, when it should be God. The apostle Paul stated that he learned how to be content (satisfied to the point where he was not disturbed) no matter what state he was in. Whether he was abounding or being abased, he remained content (see Philippians 4:11–12). Don't despair if you are not at that place of stability yet. Paul said he *learned* it and we must do the same thing.

When I came home after those ministry trips, I couldn't understand what was wrong with me. Then I finally learned that the emotional high I experienced while being involved in the excitement of the conference left me tired physically, mentally, and emotionally and I needed to rest. Like Elijah in the desert I needed to rest and recuperate.

When you experience something like that, you don't need to react as Elijah did when he was exhausted. Instead of thinking what a miserable person you are and moaning and groaning about how happy you were yesterday but how terrible you feel today and complaining to the Lord about how worthless you feel, realize what is happening. When I reach that state, I say, "Lord, I'm feeling down right now, so I'm going to rest and build myself up physically as well as spiritually. It has really helped me to be mentally prepared for both abasing and abounding in my life. We simply cannot live on an emotional high with everything in our life going exactly the way we want it to. We must have contrast in order to even appreciate the good things we have. For example, if everything in life was the same color, then no color would stand out. We can trust God to do what is best for us. I believe Paul finally came to a place of contentment because he trusted God to do what he needed in every season of his life. We greatly honor God when we make the decision to be content no matter our circumstances.

We simply cannot live on an emotional high with everything in our life going exactly the way we want it to. We must have contrast in order to even appreciate the good things we have.

CHAPTER 62

Don't Cater to Your Emotions

A young woman in one of our meetings once told me her husband was a manic-depressive. He went from one emotional extreme to another. She said for three months he would be on an emotional high and be really creative. In his business, he would buy and sell, invest large sums of money, and be tremendously successful. When he came down from those emotional highs, he would go into deep depressions that might last for as long as six months.

At one time, medical science looked at only the emotional lows for people suffering from manic depression. When they were enjoying an emotional high, nothing was done for them. According to an article I recently read, it has now been discovered that the attempt must be made to bring down the extreme highs as well. Health experts are learning that balance is the key.

We have always applauded high emotions and been critical of lows. Actually, both extreme ends are bad. Most of us will never have problems with manic depression, but we can learn a principle from how they are treated by understanding it isn't good enough to simply resist depression; we must also resist the temptation to get so emotionally high that it leaves us exhausted and open prey for the devil. None of us can live on the mountaintop all the time. There are going to be days when we are up and days when we feel down. Emotions are fickle, fluctuating frequently for no apparent reason. What we need to learn is how to manage both ends of the emotional spectrum.

I have grown in this area, and to be honest I don't feel extreme excitement now regarding my conferences or ministry opportunities. People frequently ask me if I am excited when I am leaving on a trip and they eye me suspiciously when I say, "Not really." You see, I have learned about something that is much better than mere excitement. I am *passionate* about completing the work God has given me to do. Passion is much more than a feeling. It is the fuel that causes you to finish what you start.

Since I no longer give myself over to extreme emotional highs, I don't experience the exhaustion and low moods I once did. I now have balance and it is wonderful.

One thing that is important for stable emotional health is honesty—with yourself and with others. People close to us can sense when we are struggling emotionally. I find it is best for my family and me if I am honest with them about what is going on with me. At those times when I feel myself sliding toward anger, depression, or any negative emotion, I tell my family, "My emotions are going haywire today, so if I'm quiet, just don't pay any attention to me for a while."

James 5:16 encourages us to confess our faults to one another so we may be healed and restored to a spiritual tone of mind and heart. We must remember that what we hide still has power over us, but when we bring things out in the open, they begin losing their grip immediately. If you are emotional because you are tired, just admit to yourself and others you are tired and need time to rest. Sometimes we like to think we have no limits, but the truth is only God has no limits. The rest of us need to recognize when we have done all we can and remember that is nothing to be ashamed of.

I found that if I tried to protect my spiritual reputation by pretending nothing was wrong with me, all it did was bring confusion to my entire family. They might begin to imagine I was angry with them for some reason. Then they would become upset, trying to reason out what they might have done to upset me. We were all a lot better off if I simply explained what was happening and made a decision to be quiet during those times.

When we are emotionally upset, we have a tendency to say things we regret later, so why not choose to be quiet and avoid hurting people?

One of the members of our road team who is normally very talkative and bubbly suddenly became very quiet and almost withdrawn. Several of the other team members noticed it and came to Dave and me asking what was wrong with her. They thought she was angry about something or with someone on the travel crew.

When I spoke with her, she was simply having some health problems. She had recently gone for some medical tests and was concerned while she was awaiting the results. She said, "I always get quiet and just pray when I'm dealing with something like this." I told her that getting quiet and praying was the thing to do, but that it might be good the next time to just mention to everyone that she was dealing with something personal and not to think anything about it if she seemed quiet. By being open and honest with people we can prevent the devil from placing negative things in their imaginations. People respect us if we are open and straightforward. I learned this truth with my family, and it saved all of us a lot of anxiety.

I want to remind you that the devil will try to use our emotions to bring us under guilt and condemnation, but God often uses them to test or try us so we come out of our emotional upheavals stronger and able to control them better than ever before. The key is in learning not to give in or cater to emotions. If we cater to our emotions, giving in to their every whim, we may avoid some momentary pain, but later on we suffer miserably because of all the bad decisions we made. It is always best to discipline ourselves in the beginning and then we can have long-term joy later on. I spent many years going from feeling up to feeling down, and

> The devil will try to use our emotions to bring us under guilt and condemnation, but God often uses them to test or try us so we come out of our emotional upheavals stronger and able to control them better than ever before.

expressing my negative emotions loudly and very badly. I had to learn like everyone else that it was not pleasing to God and that if I cater to my feelings now, I will always pay later. God will help you be stable if that is your desire. Pray and don't run from the hard times, because they are helping you more than you may realize.

CHAPTER 63

Don't Trust Your Feelings

Watchman Nee stated that emotion is the most formidable enemy to the life of a spiritual Christian and that he who lives by emotion lives without principle. He was expressing the apostle Paul's teaching that we cannot be spiritual—that is, walk in the Spirit—and be led by emotions.

We all have emotions. They will not go away, and we must deal with them because we cannot trust them. Emotions change frequently and often without a moment's notice. They are fickle. Emotions are one of our greatest enemies because, more than anything else, Satan uses our emotions against us to keep us from walking in the Spirit. The mind is the battlefield where the war is waged between the Spirit and the soul. I have read that when emotion pulsates, the mind becomes deceived, and conscience is denied its standard of judgment.

People often ask me, "How can I know for sure whether I'm hearing from God or from my emotions?" I believe the answer is to learn to wait. Emotions urge us toward haste. They tell us we have to do something, and we must do it right now! But godly wisdom tells us to wait until we have a clear picture of what we are to do and when we are to do it. What we all need to do is develop the capacity to back away and view our situation from God's perspective. We need to be able to make decisions based on what we *know* rather than on what we *feel*.

> We need to be able to make decisions based on what we *know* rather than on what we *feel*.

If mature Christians say, "I *feel* God wants me to do this or that," in reality what they are saying is they sense in their spirit the Lord is telling them to do or not do something. They are not talking about operating by their emotions, but by what they perceive spiritually to be the will of God for them in that situation. Whenever we are faced with a decision, we need to ask ourselves: "Am I making this decision according to my fleshly feelings or according to what I feel deep in my spirit which is the will of God?"

CHAPTER 64

Emotional Discernment

My husband Dave and I have a certain way we handle our money. At one time we each got a weekly allowance. I usually saved my money to buy clothes and other things I wanted or needed.

One time I had about $375 saved to buy a good watch. I always had cheaper watches and really wanted to buy a good, 14-karat gold watch, so the band would not discolor.

Because I had been shopping for a watch for a while and discovered that the type I wanted would cost about eight or nine hundred dollars, I was saving my money toward that goal.

One day Dave and I were in the mall and happened to stop at a jewelry store where I saw a watch that was only gold-plated but was really very pretty. It matched my ring and seemed to be just what I was looking for. It fit my arm perfectly, so it wouldn't need adjustment. Not only that, the clerk offered to mark it down from $395 to $316. So my emotions said, "Yes! That's exactly what I want!"

But then my husband said, "Well, now, you know, it's not 14-karat gold."

So I asked the clerk, "How long do you think the gold-plating will last?"

"Well, it could last from five to ten years." Notice she wasn't making any real commitment; she just said it might last that long.

I turned to Dave and said, "Oh, my. I really like that watch. What should I do?"

"It's your money," he answered.

"I'll tell you what I'm going to do," I told the clerk. "You hold it for me for half an hour. I'm going to walk around the mall for a bit. If I want the watch, I'll come back within thirty minutes."

So Dave and I walked around the mall for a while. As we did so, we passed a dress shop. Because I needed a couple of new outfits, I went in and found a really nice suit. I tried it on, and it fit perfectly. I loved it.

"That's a nice suit," Dave said. "You really ought to get it."

I looked at the price tag and saw that it read $279. That was more than I usually paid for clothing at that time, but I really wanted that suit! I was trying to decide what to do and became very confused, so I put the suit back on the rack.

"Aren't you going to buy it?" David asked.

"No," I answered. "I'm not going to buy it either. I'm going to think about it."

Actually there were three things I wanted. I wanted the watch, I wanted the suit, and I wanted not to be broke. I wanted to have some money on hand to buy little things I needed from time to time and to be able to do some things I enjoyed like taking my kids out for lunch now and then.

What did I eventually do? I applied wisdom. I decided to wait. The watch would have taken all my savings and would still not be what I really wanted. The suit was beautiful, but it also would have taken most of my savings. Since it was long-sleeved, I wouldn't have been able to wear it until the next fall. It would have hung in my closet for a long time.

The best thing, I decided, was to keep my money and wait until I was sure what I wanted most.

I really learned a lesson from that experience. I had peace about my decision. As much as I would have enjoyed either the watch or the suit, I knew I had done the right thing.

It turned out that my husband later used his saved allowance and bought both the watch and the suit for me—plus a ring to match! It all worked out beautifully because I was willing to listen to reason and apply wisdom rather than being controlled by my emotions.

If we are willing to learn to control our emotions, God will bless us.

> If we are willing to learn to control our emotions, God will bless us.

I am not saying that if you will delay every decision, someone else will make it for you and you will get everything you want and more. I *am* saying that usually the wisest course is: when in doubt, don't!

When faced with any difficult decision, wait until you have peace or a clear answer before taking a step you may regret. Emotions are wonderful, but they must not be allowed to take precedence over wisdom and knowledge. Remember: control your emotions; don't let them control you.

CHAPTER 65

Managing Your Emotions for a Life of Joy and Peace

It is always fun to go to banquets or other catered events where all your wants and needs are met immediately and fully by someone else. But there is always a price to be paid for that kind of service. The same is true in the area of emotions. There is a price we must pay for catering to the desires and demands of our emotions—the demands of our flesh. Romans 8:8 explains, "So then those who are living the life of the flesh [catering to the appetites and impulses of their carnal nature] cannot please or satisfy God, or be acceptable to Him."

Following the desires of the flesh leads to destruction; following the Spirit leads to life and peace (see v. 6). If we follow the dictates and demands of our flesh—our unbridled emotions—we will have a price to pay. Why? The thoughts and purposes of the flesh are hostile to God and cannot submit to God's law (see v. 7). Part of the price we must pay for catering to our emotions is not being able to live the Spirit-filled life. The flesh is opposed to the Spirit, and the Spirit is opposed to the flesh. They are continually antagonistic to each other. This means we cannot be led by our emotions and still be led by the Holy Spirit. We have to make a choice.

We cannot be led by our emotions and still be led by the Holy Spirit. We have to make a choice.

When the Bible says those who cater to their emotions cannot please or satisfy God or be acceptable to Him, it does not mean God doesn't love them. You and I can be in a terrible emotional mess and still be loved by our heavenly Father. Having emotional problems will not keep us from going to heaven. It just means God is not pleased with our lifestyle. It puts Him in a position in which He cannot do for us all He would like to do.

We all want our children to be blessed and to share in our inheritance, but we are not inclined to entrust our inheritance to one of our children who chooses to follow a lifestyle of unbridled sensuality. God is not pleased with those who live by the flesh rather than by His Spirit because He cannot trust them with His best. God still loves us, but He wants to be able to give us the best He has for us in the new life He provided for us in Jesus.

Allowing our emotions to lead our decisions will definitely prevent us from having a life filled with peace and joy. Emotional decisions always create trouble sooner or later and we live in turmoil because of them. The decisions we make today will provoke circumstances we must deal with tomorrow. If I lose my temper and make an emotional decision to quit my job because my boss makes me angry, then I may end up with a lot of stress a week from now when I need to pay my bills and don't have an income.

Hebrews 12 says no discipline for the present seems joyous, but later on it yields the peaceful fruit of righteousness. The law of God's kingdom is that we always reap what we sow. If we choose to sow discipline and right choices, we will reap a life of joy and peace. However, if we sow emotional choices, we will reap a life of turmoil and sadness. God sets before every person life and death and He instructs us to choose life. Since we all have the privilege of free choice, we must take responsibility for our lives and no longer blame circumstances and other people for all the things that go wrong. It is very simple: if we make enough right choices, we will have a life filled with peace and joy!

CHAPTER 66

One Step at a Time

Healing of emotional wounds is a process, not something that takes place all at once or overnight. It requires an investment of time and diligent obedience to God's commands. I realize from my own experience that it often seems that no progress is being made at all. You may feel you have so many problems you are not getting anywhere. But you are!

You have to keep in mind that even though you have a long way to go, you have also come a long way. The solution is to thank God for the progress you have made so far and to trust Him to lead you on to eventual victory—one step at a time. If you are reading this book and happen to be someone who has spent your life making wrong choices and you feel you have never made any progress at all, then you can get started today changing things in your life by making right choices!

In my oral presentations on this subject I like to hold up several different colored shoestrings tied together in a knot. I tell my audience, "This is you when you first start the process of transformation with God. You're all knotted up. Each knot represents a different problem in your life. Untangling those knots and straightening out those problems is going to take a bit of time and effort, so don't get discouraged if it doesn't happen all at once."

All of us have many similar problems, but God doesn't deal with all of them at the same time or all of us in the same way. The Lord may be dealing with one person about anger or bitterness, somebody else about selfishness, and someone else about another area completely.

If you want to receive emotional healing from God and come

into an area of wholeness, you must realize that healing is a process and allow the Lord to deal with you and your problems in His own way and in His own time. Your part is to cooperate with Him in whatever area He chooses to start dealing with you first. You may want to work on one thing, and God may want to start with something else. If you pursue your own agenda, you will soon learn that God's power is not available for that problem. The grace (power and goodness) of God is not there to deliver you outside of His will and timing.

I tell people in my seminars, "Being convicted by the message you hear in this meeting doesn't mean you are to go out and set up some kind of ten point plan for dealing with that situation. First you must pray and ask God to begin to work in that area of your life. Then you must cooperate with Him as He does it." We do need to make decisions and be people of action, but we must also remember that Jesus said, "Apart from Me you can do nothing (John 15:5)." In the world everyone seeks to be independent, but in God's economy we must all learn to be totally dependent on Him.

In the world everyone seeks to be independent, but in God's economy we must all learn to be totally dependent on Him.

As God deals with each of us in one specific area at a time, it may take anywhere from one hour to several years. In my own case, the Lord dealt with me for one solid year to get me to understand He loves me. I will never forget it. I needed that foundation in my life. I desperately needed to know how much God loved me personally, not just when I did what I thought I was supposed to do, but all the time—whether I "deserved" His love or not. I needed to know God loved me unconditionally and His love was not something I could buy with works or good behavior.

As part of the process, I began to get up every morning saying, "God loves me!" Even when I did something wrong, I would say, "God loves me!" When I would have trials or problems, I would say it, again and again: "God loves me!" Every time Satan tried to steal my assurance of that love, I would say it over and over: "God loves me! He loves me!" I read books about God's unconditional, unending love. I studied all the scripture I could find on God's love. I dwelled on it continually until I had that foundational truth firmly imbedded in my mind and heart: "God loves me!" Through the process of continual study and meditation in this area, I became rooted and grounded in God's love as the apostle Paul encourages us to do in Ephesians 3.

One of our problems is in our modern, instantaneous society we tend to jump from one thing to another. We have come to expect everything to be quick and easy. We won't stick with a problem until we see a breakthrough and know we have victory in that area.

The Lord is not like that. He never gets in a hurry, and He never quits. He will deal with us about one particular thing, and then He will let us rest for a while—but not too long. Soon He will come back and begin to work on something else. He will continue until, one by one, our knots are all untied. It may be hard, and it may take time, but if you will stick with the program, sooner or later you will see the victory and experience the freedom you have wanted so long. I finally learned to be excited about what God was doing in my life, rather than dreading it. When I initially began my walk with God and He dealt with me about a problem I had, I often thought, *Oh no, not another thing that is wrong with me!* I eventually learned that God dealing with me was a sign of His love for me. He loves us too much to leave us the way we are.

Let God be God in your life and don't forget to enjoy the journey. The important thing to remember is: no matter how long it takes, never give up, and never quit!

CHAPTER 67

Keep Pressing Forward

The main thing God asks or requires we do to bring about the answer to our problems is to believe and keep pressing on. Study the Word of God and spend time with Him. If part or all of our lives are in knots, we may not be able to untie it ourselves. The simple truth is we need God's help. Some issues in life will be harder to deal with than others, and if we merely try to take care of things ourselves we often end up making matters worse.

At one time in my life I became so entangled in my problems and my futile efforts to untangle them, I was no good to myself or anybody else. I was extremely frustrated most of the time and quite confused. I felt I was really *trying* to change and that nothing *I* did was working. Then I learned from scripture that God will frustrate us if we are not leaning on Him.

> For God sets Himself against the proud (the insolent, the overbearing, the disdainful, the presumptuous, the boastful)—[and He opposes, frustrates, and defeats them], but gives grace (favor, blessing) to the humble (1 Peter 5:5).

Once I learned to let the Lord handle the problems and just cooperate with Him, things began to work much better. Now I enjoy a life of freedom in Jesus and am able to help others who are as bound and tangled as I was.

When God convicts you of a problem in your personality or life, just agree with Him. Ask for His forgiveness and be willing to change, but realize you cannot change without His help. Ask Him to change you rather than *trying* to change yourself. God works in our lives as we place our trust and confidence in Him, not as we struggle to do things ourselves.

God works in our lives as we place our trust and confidence in Him, not as we struggle to do things ourselves.

We all need help in some way or another, and that is nothing to be ashamed of. There are many people who have been severely damaged emotionally. I have a feeling most of us at one time have been or will be part of that group in one way or another. Some people experience feelings of unworthiness. They have a shame-based self-hatred, a sense of self-rejection, an inner voice telling them they are no good, that something is wrong with them. For years I walked around with the nagging thought, *What's wrong with me?*

When we are born again, the first thing the Lord wants to give us is His righteousness through His blood so we can stop asking what's wrong with us and start believing that something is right with us now that we are in Christ. Perfectionists are always trying to prove their worth and gain love and acceptance through performance. These people always struggle to do a little bit better in the hope someone will love and accept them more.

Still others are supersensitive. The apostle Paul said one of the characteristics of love is "it is not touchy" (1 Corinthians 13:5). Are you touchy? Would you like to be delivered? If so, part of the answer is to face the fact that if you are touchy, the problem is not with those who constantly offend you or hurt your feelings, but it is with you and your supersensitive nature. Being secure in Christ will heal you and keep you from getting your feelings hurt constantly.

One of the things that helped me in this area was a simple statement made to me years ago by a lady who was reading a book on this subject. She told me, "You know, the book I'm reading says that 95 percent of the time when people hurt your feelings, they didn't intend to do so." That means if you get your feelings hurt easily the reason is you choose to. The good news is you can also choose not to. When you lay aside supersensitivity, you will feel so much better about yourself and others! I know. My feelings used to get hurt if my husband didn't do something I thought he ought to do to show he loved and appreciated me or if he failed to compliment me when I thought he ought to. I now have confidence that he loves me, and I don't pressure him all the time to prove it.

If you walk into a room and don't get the attention you think you deserve, do you get hurt? Do you feel others don't esteem you the way they should? It is interesting that people who are supersensitive about what others do to them are often totally insensitive to what they do to others. If you see yourself in any of these things I am describing, you need to place that problem into God's hands and let Him do the work in you that needs to be done. It has helped me tremendously over the past few years to place myself into God's hands and let Him work out things for the best. I try to abandon myself to Him and trust Him to bring me what He wants me to have. I am learning not to look to other people to meet my needs, but rather to look to the Lord to fulfill my needs, as He knows best for me.

Be patient with yourself and always remember that God loves you unconditionally; and when He shows you something that needs to change, it is intended to help you and never to make you feel bad about yourself. We all have problems and areas in our lives that need to change. The most important thing is we press on! If you are willing to do that then God will see your heart and be pleased.

CHAPTER 68

God Wants to Heal Past Hurts Affecting Your Present

Many times people are supersensitive because they have been hurt in the past, so their bruised emotions are easily pained. That's why they are so touchy. I was that way. I was hard to get along with because I was so insecure. Like many people, because I did not get the love I needed for much of my life, I kept trying to get other people to make me happy. When I married, I became a "suffocator." Because love and affection had been denied to me, I tended to require too much out of anyone who showed me any fondness or attention at all.

I learned that in a marriage relationship, we must allow our partner some liberty. We must get rid of the fear of what the person may think of us and develop instead a reverential fear and awe of God. Why do some of us have such a tremendous fear of what somebody else thinks of us? The reason is we have a poor self-image. Do we become any less valuable or worthy in the eyes of God because of someone else's negative opinion of us? Of course not, but we feel less valuable unless we are secure in who we are in Christ. People who have a great deal of fear of others are good candidates to become controlled by someone who likes to control others.

Many times people who suffer from poor self-esteem allow themselves to be controlled by someone who promises to show them love or acceptance. They allow themselves to be manipulated like a puppet on a string. They are afraid to break the string because they are fearful of losing the attention they receive from the controller. They fear loneliness and the feeling of being rejected.

Then there are those who, because of emotional hurts, become controllers and manipulators themselves. I was like that at one time in my life. When I married, because of my past hurts I had a very hard time submitting to my husband in the Lord, as the Bible teaches (see Ephesians 5:22; Colossians 3:18). I was afraid if I submitted to him and allowed him to exercise any control over me, he would hurt me. I always tried to stay in control of every situation due to the fear of being taken advantage of.

Dave kept telling me, "Joyce, I'm not going to hurt you! Don't you understand that I love you and that the decisions I make are made with your best interest in mind? But for a long time I couldn't see that. I couldn't imagine anybody caring enough for me to make decisions that would benefit me in any way. I thought if I allowed him to exercise any degree of control over my life, he would take advantage of me and do what was best for him, not for me. There are people who will do that, but Dave was not one of them. It is not right for us to punish everyone for what one bad person may have done to us in the past. I finally had to make a decision to trust and just believe God would vindicate me if people treated me unjustly.

We tend to bring our past wounds into our new relationships. One of the things God wants to do for us is help us learn to function in the new relationships we have developed, rather than ruin them because of the bad past experiences. We must approach every day as a new day with new opportunities. We must choose to let go of the past because our future has no room for the disappointment of the past. To go on we must let go!

Many people who are hurt inside develop addictive behaviors—alcoholism, drug addictions, food addictions, spending addictions, and on and on. If you suffer from any of these types of bondages, God wants to heal you. He wants to heal you from a sense of unworthiness, from shame and self-hatred and self-rejection, from addictive behaviors, from supersensitivity and fear and the labor of trying to be perfect in your own strength. God can heal you everywhere you hurt! One time the Lord showed me, "Joyce, I'm not nearly as hard to please as people think I am." God does not require you and me to be perfect immediately; He just wants us to keep growing. If we could be perfect, it would not have been necessary for God to send Jesus, the Perfect Sacrifice, for us. God has the marvelous ability to love us in the midst of our imperfections so why not just believe that and relax! When a person receives Jesus as his Savior and Lord He begins a work of healing in him. He does it inside and it shows on the outside. For example, the more we know God loves us, the more confident we will be in all our dealings with other people. If we have fear in our hearts, it always shows up in some way. Even if we pretend we are afraid of nothing, it always comes out. It is very important that you understand you are on a journey and will not completely reach your destination until your time here on earth is over and you go to heaven to live with God there for eternity. The Bible says when He calls us home we will all be changed in the twinkling of an eye. Anything still wrong with us at that point will be instantly fixed (see 1 Corinthians 15:52). But until then we just need to keep our eyes on Jesus and sincerely do the best we can every day and trust God with our whole hearts. No matter how you feel, God is working in you and bringing you into a place of wholeness. Jesus came to seek and save that which was lost and that includes everything the devil has stolen from us. Don't look at your journey as a burden, but as an exciting opportunity to reach new heights every single day you live.

God does not require you and me to be perfect immediately; He just wants us to keep growing.

CHAPTER 69

Your Answer Is Under Your Nose

There is no subject in the Bible we should take more seriously than the mouth—the words we speak. I do not believe anyone can live in victory without being well informed concerning the power of words. The mouth can be used to bring blessing or destruction not only to our own lives, but also to the lives of others. Proverbs 18:21 states, "Death and life are in the power of the tongue, and they who indulge in it shall eat the fruit of it [for death or life]."

> The mouth can be used to bring blessing or destruction not only to our own lives, but also to the lives of others.

If you are dealing with problems, your answer may be right under your nose. At least a major part of it could be. Usually when we have mountains of problems in our lives we talk *about* them, but God's Word instructs us to talk *to* them, as we see in a passage when Jesus said that we are to speak to our mountain in faith, commanding it to be lifted up and thrown into the sea (Mark 11:23, 24). This is a radical statement and one that deserves some study.

First of all, what do we say to the mountains in our lives? It is obvious we are not to hurl our will at them, but the will of God, and His will is His Word.

In Luke 4 when Jesus was being tempted by Satan in the wilderness, He answered every trial with the Word of God. He repeatedly said, "It is written," and quoted Scriptures that met the lies and deceptions of the devil head on. Many of us have a tendency to try this for a while, but when we do not see quick results, we stop speaking the

Word to our problems and return to speaking our feelings, which is probably what got us into trouble to begin with.

A stonecutter may strike a rock ninety-nine times with a hammer, and there may be no evidence at all that the rock is cracking. Then on the one hundredth time, it may split in half. Each blow was weakening the stone even though there were no signs to indicate it.

Persistence is a vital link to victory. We must know what we believe and be determined to stick with it until we see results.

Knowing, speaking and obeying the Word of God is powerful and absolutely necessary in overcoming life's problems. Obedience is the central theme of the Bible. For many of us, our life is in a mess due to disobedience. The disobedience may have been the result of ignorance or rebellion, but the only way out of the mess is repentance and a return to submission and obedience.

If a person thinks he can live in disobedience, but speak God's Word to his mountains and see results, he will be sadly disappointed. Jesus' teaching in Mark 11:22–26, the passage in which He discusses speaking to the mountain, He also talks about releasing faith. Jesus said to constantly have faith in God; He spoke of prayer and the importance of praying prayers of believing. He gave a command to forgive and stated plainly if we do not forgive, neither will our Father in heaven forgive us our failings and shortcomings.

Multitudes of people who have accepted Christ as their personal Savior fall into the deception of trying to operate one of God's principles while completely ignoring another. Confessing the word of God is a positive principal that will bring good results, but unforgiveness is a negative principal that weakens our walk with God. When we mix positives and negatives we make no progress. I strongly encourage you to do your best to obey God in all things, not just the ones that are convenient to you at a particular time. We must do right when it is easy or hard, convenient or inconvenient. Obedience produces wonderful results, and it is the adjustment to all inharmonious circumstances in our life.

CHAPTER 70

Speaking God's Language

The Bible teaches us we can have what we say. To clarify, what we say *must* line up with God's Word expressed in the Bible and His will for us at that particular time in our lives. "Speaking to our mountains" is not a magic charm or incantation we pull out and use when we are in trouble or when we want something for ourselves, while we continue in carnality and a disobedient lifestyle.

As long as you and I are carnal (living by our lusts and selfish desires), we should hope and pray for God *not* to give us what we say. As immature Christians what we think we want is not usually the thing that will be the best for us. We will be saying a lot of things that are our will and not God's will, simply because we cannot tell the difference yet. As "babies in Christ," we simply do not know how to talk yet, which is what the apostle Paul told the Corinthians (1 Corinthians 3:3).

It seems to me from my years in ministry and observations in the Kingdom of God, believers, even teachers of the Word, have a difficult time with balance. The doctrine concerning the power of words, the mouth, confession, calling those things that be not as though they are, and speaking things into existence, is one example in which I have seen people get off into extremes. It seems the flesh wants to live in the ditch on one side of the road or the other, but it has a difficult time staying in the middle of the highway between the lines of safety.

Extremes are actually the devil's playground. If he cannot get a believer to totally ignore a truth and live in deception, his next tactic will be to get him so one-sided and out of balance with that truth he is no better off than he was before. Sometimes he is even worse off than he was.

Wisdom is a central theme of God's Word. As a matter of fact, there is no real victory without it. I have dealt with many people over the years, both lay people and those in full-time ministry, who simply do not use any common sense. Wisdom does not operate in extremes. Wisdom is full of prudence, and prudence is good management. I believe we might say that wisdom is a combination of balance, common sense, and good judgment.

> Wisdom is a combination of balance, common sense, and good judgment.

I believe very strongly in the power of speaking in line with God's Word, also referred to as confessing God's Word. I believe we should speak to our mountains, and I believe that in many, if not most instances the answer to our problems is definitely right under our nose (in our mouth). But I also believe very strongly in the maturity of the believer, the crucifixion of the fleshly nature by choosing to make the right decisions to follow the spirit, dying to selfishness, and the necessity for obedience and submission to the Holy Spirit.

Most teachers have a particular "bent" to their teaching—and rightfully so. It has to do with the call of God on their lives. Some are called to exhort and keep the children of God cheered up, to keep them zealous and pressing forward. Others may be called to teach faith, and still others prosperity. There are those who are called to teach almost exclusively on finances. Many have been called to teach and demonstrate healing. However, no matter what our particular passion is, those of us who teach God's Word must teach the whole counsel of God's Word and not lean so much toward one area that others are totally ignored. New believers, especially, should guard against becoming lopsided toward a particular teaching and remember to stay balanced to avoid falling into one of the devil's ditches of extremes. However, mature believers should also guard against gravitating toward extremes.

The point is to learn how to cooperate with the Holy Spirit to see the will of God accomplished in our lives. Give your ear to wisdom. Follow God's system of "checks and balances" to help you stay balanced—assembling with other believers, seeking godly counsel rather than the wisdom of the world, for example. Your new way of living requires you stay on the narrow path, staying centered, not being swayed either to the right or the left ditch, keeping your eyes right on Jesus.

CHAPTER 71

The Effect of Words

The earth God created was not made from materials that could be seen. Genesis 1 tells us God spoke, and things began to appear: light, sky, earth, vegetation, plants yielding seed, and trees bearing fruit; the sun, moon, and stars; fish and birds; every kind of living creature: livestock, creeping things, wild beasts, and domestic animals. The earth and everything in it were all created out of nothing that could be seen and are today upheld by nothing that can be seen.

In Hebrews 1:3 we read that God is "...upholding and maintaining and guiding and propelling the universe by His mighty word of power...." The universe that was created by His mighty words is still being upheld today by the same thing.

You might say, "Well, sure, Joyce, but that is God."

But we must remember we are created in God's image (Genesis 1:26, 27), and we are supposed to act like Him.

Paul stated we are to imitate God, to follow His example, see Ephesians 5:1. In Romans 4:17 we read that God "...gives life to the dead and speaks of the non-existent things that [He has foretold and promised] as if they [already] existed."

God's Word is His promise to us, and we should speak of those things He promised us as if they already existed.

Over thirty years ago God taught me the importance of speaking His word out loud. He told me that I needed to stop saying negative things and start saying positive things. I made sure my confessions were backed up by God's Word. I wasn't confessing that I would be the President or CEO of General Motors, but I was confessing that

I would fulfill my destiny. I declared that I walked in love and all the other fruit of the Spirit. I claimed good health, prosperity, godly character, wisdom, generosity, and about 60 other things God placed on my heart. Today, all of those things are a reality in my life and I am still growing. We cannot expect to experience God's best if we are going to constantly verbally disagree with His Word. Remember, the answer to many of your problems is right under your nose. What have you been saying lately? How do you talk when you are having challenges in life, or when you feel the pressures of daily life? When Jesus like a lamb was being led to slaughter (when He died on the cross) the Bible says that He opened not His mouth. This is very significant because to me it indicates that Jesus realized He was better off to be quiet than to say the wrong thing. He knew the power of words!

Jesus realized He was better off to be quiet than to say the wrong thing. He knew the power of words!

We all have angels assigned to help us, but the Bible says they hearken (listen) to the word of God. An angel is not going to assist us because we complain all day. They won't assist us due to our fearful, negative speech. Start saying what the Bible says you can have instead of just talking about your circumstances. If you will I believe that over time you will be amazed at the positive difference in your life. If you are anything like the rest of us I am sure you have tried being negative and seen the results, so why not give God's way an opportunity. He has blessings piled up just waiting for you to learn how to talk right!

CHAPTER 72

Exchanging Fear for Faith

We all know what fear feels like. It is tormenting and prevents our progress. Fear can cause us to shake, perspire, feel weak, and run from things we should face.

We should have a type of reverential fear of God we call "holy fear." It is a respectful fear of God that causes us to walk in obedience to Him because we know He is powerful and we should always do as He says. It is a right fear that realizes God means what He says and our lives always work out best if we follow His instructions.

There is also what I will term a "normal" fear that helps us in some situations. The purpose for feeling the fear described above is for "fight or flight" in emergencies. Sometimes we need the instant alertness and enormous boost of energy to handle immediate potentially dangerous situations. For example, I once had a friend who had a teenage son who suddenly had a convulsion. She lived about three blocks from a hospital and without even thinking about what she was doing, she picked up her son who was larger than her and carried him the three blocks. Her body produced extra adrenaline that enabled her to do something she could not have done normally. In this instance the fear she felt was a good thing.

But many people live daily with fear that is not from God but is Satan's tool to prevent us from living the good life God has for us. Second Timothy 1:7 tells us God has not given us the spirit of fear; He has given us a spirit of power, love, and a sound, well-balanced mind.

God wants us to live in faith. Faith is the leaning of our entire personalities on Him with absolute trust and confidence in His power, wisdom, and goodness. It is the evidence of things we do not see and the conviction of their reality.

Faith operates in the spiritual realm. Many people are accustomed to believing only in things they can see and feel, but as children of God, to live in the fullness of the new life God intends, we learn to become comfortable living in the spiritual realm, one we cannot see. We don't see God because He is a Spirit, but we believe firmly in Him. We don't usually see angels, but God's Word says they are all around us protecting us. By believing in God and His Word and releasing our faith in Him to do as He promises in His Word, we can reach into the spiritual realm and pull things out into visual reality God wants us to enjoy.

As children of God, to live in the fullness of the new life God intends, we learn to become comfortable living in the spiritual realm, one we cannot see.

Satan delights in calling our attention to circumstances opposing the promises of God we know to be true in an attempt to make us fearful of the future. God, however, wants us to trust our present and future to Him and believe He is greater than any circumstance or threat from the devil. Great examples of men and women in desperate circumstances with fear filling their hearts who decided to put their faith in God appear throughout the Bible. The Bible gives us the many different accounts of the glorious deliverances each person experienced.

Once you become a Christian, you can still live your life being tormented by fears of all kinds unless you decide to live by faith. You must decide whether you will live in fear or in faith. You received Jesus as your Savior by faith; the next step is to learn to live by faith. It is the matter of the practice of making right choices, in other words, choosing faith in each situation that tries to bring fear to you. After you make the right choice, you may still feel fear trying to take you over, but despite the feeling, keep moving forward and taking the action corresponding with your decision.

Courage is not the absence of fear, but it is taking action in the presence of it. When God told His servants not to fear, He wasn't commanding them not to feel fear; He was telling them to be obedient to Him no matter how they felt. God knows the spirit of fear will always try to keep us from making progress in our walk with Him. He reminds us over and over in His Word, He is always with us; He will not fail or forsake us, and we do not have to bow down to fear.

Eleanor Roosevelt said, "You gain strength, courage and confidence by every experience in which you really stop to look fear in the face. You must do the thing you think you cannot do."

Only faith pleases God. We receive from God through faith. It is of utmost importance for the new believer in Christ to learn about faith and begin walking in it. Developing strong faith is done just like developing strong muscles: you exercise your faith little by little and each time you do it gets stronger.

Matthew 17:20 teaches us that all things are possible to him who believes. Even little faith can move mountains of trouble in our lives. If you have spent your life trying to solve all your own problems and have often felt frustrated and disappointed, you are on the brink of a new experience. In inviting God to become involved in everything concerning you, you will find what is impossible with man is possible with God. According to our faith, it will be done for us (see Matthew 9:29).

If you have lived in fear, it is good to know you can begin exchanging fear for faith in God. Remember all this learning of new ways takes time. Don't be discouraged and give up. Everything in the earth works according to the law of gradual growth. Little by little everything changes if we keep doing what God tells us to do. As we grow in understanding the depth of God's love for us and the realization we have been made right with God through the death and resurrection of Jesus, little by little we find it easier and easier to walk in faith.

CHAPTER 73

Enjoying Life

Many people have difficulty accepting this fact: They are free to enjoy their lives. The devil has done a good job of deceiving them. But the truth is Jesus came to free us from bondage; He came to give us the power to live life in abundance to the full, to the point of overflowing. It is God's will for us to enjoy our lives. Not everything will go just as we would like; we will still have difficulties. But enjoying life does mean we can rise above the misery in the world and share a resurrected life through Jesus and through the power of the Holy Spirit. It means we can enjoy life even while we are having difficulty or challenges in our own lives.

People who think knowing God is only a relationship involving following a set of rules have no idea how wonderful life can be for the person living in true relationship with and for God. God is our real life. In Him we live and move and have our being. Learning to enjoy God releases us to enjoy every single day of our lives.

Enjoy fellowship with Him. God is concerned about anything that concerns you, and the Bible actually says God will perfect what concerns you. He is working in your life at all times, bringing you more completely into His will.

Don't be afraid of God in a wrong way. It is true we should have a reverential fear of God, respecting Him and knowing He is all-powerful and means what He says. But we should never be afraid of God becoming angry with us every time we make a mistake or of punishing us every time we fail to be perfect. God is merciful and slow to anger. He is long-suffering and knows our makeup. He understands our weaknesses and infirmities.

If you are like many other people, you have a number of areas in your life and personality needing change, and God will change them. But, the good news is you can enjoy God and enjoy your life while He is transforming those areas.

Although your life right now may not be the type of life you see for yourself in God, it is the only one you have at the present time. You need to start enjoying it! Find the good things in it. Accentuate the positive and learn to see the good in everything. Enjoy your family and friends. Don't pick them apart and spend most of your time being very busy trying to change them. Pray for them and let God do the changing.

Although your life right now may not be the type of life you see for yourself in God, it is the only one you have at the present time. You need to start enjoying it!

Enjoy your work, enjoy your home, and enjoy ordinary, everyday life. This is possible if you trust God and decide to have a good attitude. Keep your eyes on God and not everything wrong with you, your life, your family, and the world. God has a good plan for you, and He is already starting to work in you to transform you even though you may not yet be able to see outward results. Go ahead and rejoice ahead of time in looking forward to the good things to come.

Most people live believing they cannot enjoy their lives as long as they have problems. This is wrong thinking and does not reflect the way God thinks. Don't waste your life and energy dwelling on the mistakes or regrets of your past. Continue thinking about the great new future you have through Jesus Christ, and all He already has available to you, an inheritance you are only beginning to understand. You can enjoy whatever you decide to enjoy. You can enjoy sitting in a traffic jam if you decide to. Remember, this is a new way of thinking and living that God has for you to practice.

I finally learned to enjoy where I am while I am on the way to where I am going and I strongly urge you to do the same. There is much for God to do in your life for your benefit and for the benefit of those you know and influence, and He does not want you to be miserable while He is doing it. Just as babies must grow into adults, Christians must also grow. It is a process that often takes longer than we desire, but there is no point in not enjoying the journey.

Continuing to remind yourself God does not expect you to be perfect today will help you avoid spending days under guilt and condemnation after you make a mistake. God already knows you will never be completely perfect as long as you live on the earth. He does expect each of us to keep pressing on by sincerely doing our best every day to serve Him. When we keep practicing the new behaviors of our new way of thinking and living, we will eventually replace our old behaviors with the new ones as our lifestyle. Admitting our failures, asking for forgiveness for our sins, and being willing to turn from them is a big part. If we will do this, God will do the rest. He will keep working with us through His Holy Spirit. He will teach us, change us, and use us.

When you step out into a new way of living, I believe you will never be sorry. Enjoy God, enjoy yourself, and enjoy the life Jesus died to give you!

SECTION III

Your Body—Your Home, God's Home

CHAPTER 74

Your Body Affects Your Spiritual Life

Receiving Jesus as your Savior or receiving a special touch from God may be a starting place, but then we need to grow in God. Spiritual growth is not always easy, but it is necessary. The Holy Spirit will guide us by helping us see the things that need to change in our lives. He will also help us by teaching us God's Word if we will be diligent to study it. A Christian absolutely must learn the Word of God if they are going to enjoy the new life God has provided in Christ.

The Bible says if we continue in God's Word we will be His disciples and we will know the truth and it will make us free (see John 8:31–32 KJV). The word "continue" is a key word in these verses. It is not what we do wrong once that messes up our lives and it is not what we do right once that fixes them. We must "diligently" seek God and then He rewards us (see Hebrews 11:6). If we continue to study God's Word, we will be transformed into His image (see 2 Corinthians 3:18).

Growth is a process, not an event, and the sooner we realize that the more we can enjoy the journey. Unrealistic expectations are the root cause of much unhappiness. If we expect to receive Jesus as our Savior and have everything perfect right away, we are setting ourselves up for much disappointment. However, if we realize growth is a process and will take time, we are more likely to finish the journey.

As long as we are on earth we will always be changing and growing, and that is exciting to me. I am a goal-oriented person, meaning I always like to have something to look forward to. Spiritual growth can be exciting if we learn to look at it properly. When the Holy Spirit convicts you of some area in your life that needs to change, realize that is His way of showing His love for you. He wants us to improve and be the best we can be because He knows that every change we make to be more like Him will release new levels of joy into our lives.

As we study God's Word, our eyes are opened to see things previously hidden in our lives. Things that were there all along, but we were blind to them. God's Word is light, and we should never be afraid to live in the light.

When God shows us things that need to change in our lives, we should never feel condemned or ashamed. Remember that what you are seeing for the first time, God knew was there all along. God is not surprised by our faults, He knew all about them long before we did and He loves us unconditionally. We should be repentant, which means we are sorry for our sins and willing to turn away from them to a new way of living, but feeling guilty and condemned does no good at all. It actually presses us down and steals the energy we need to work with God for improvement.

When God brings something to light in your life that will need to be changed by His power, all He wants us to do is agree with Him and ask Him to change it. While God is changing us, His love remains the same. When our behavior improves, He does not love us any more than He ever did before.

It is difficult to be enthusiastic and passionate about anything if we feel tired all the time.

One of the things God will ultimately deal with every person about is how they take care of their body, because the body has a profound effect on the spirit. We should do everything we can do to be as healthy as possible. It is difficult to be enthusiastic and passionate about anything if we feel tired all the time.

It is a mistake to think God only deals with us about spiritual things. As I have said, we are a tri-part being—spirit, soul, and body—and all three are very important to God. He wants to work through our entire being. The apostle Paul prayed for the Ephesians that the Holy Spirit would fill their personalities (see Ephesians 3:16) and he also prayed that they would be bodies wholly filled with God Himself (see Ephesians 3:19). God is interested in our entire being, and we should be also.

There are many things that can contribute to poor health, but one of them is trying so hard to please people that we end up placing unreasonable stress on ourselves. We all have limits and that means we will have times when we need to say no. Anytime someone wants to hear yes and we tell them no, they probably won't like it, but we must follow God, not man. Trying to keep all the people happy all the time is just too hard. If that is our goal in life, we will certainly wear ourselves out.

We all need to live with margins. That means we should leave time in between commitments for prayer, Bible study, rest, relaxation, and fun. If we merely run from thing to thing with no margin between, we will have poor personal relationships, poor health, and a poverty-stricken spiritual life.

I urge you to make a decision to live a balanced life and realize that every aspect of your being is vitally important. Take care of your spirit, mind, emotions, and body. It is not wrong to take care of yourself... it is God's will for your new life!

CHAPTER 75

Taking Care of Your Body—Get Some Sleep!

Taking care of our bodies is very important, because they are God's house. There are several simple things we can do to ensure better health and increased energy. A nutritionist I work with said one of the most important things for any person to do in taking care of the body is to sleep seven or eight hours every night and drink lots of water. Some people mistreat their bodies by never getting enough sleep and eating excessive junk foods such as donuts, sodas, candy bars, and potato chips. Those same people when they get really sick usually pray and ask God for healing. God is merciful and He is our Healer, but He also expects us to live a balanced lifestyle and use common sense. Our bodies are a precious, marvelous gift from God, and we should respect them and take good care of them.

If we worry excessively, dwelling on problems instead of spending time thinking about God's promises in His Word, we may experience a negative effect on our heath. Excessive, long-term stress of any kind eventually has an adverse effect on our bodies and can be the root cause of many diseases. We must understand that if we wear out our bodies, we don't have a spare to pull out of a closet somewhere and use! We cannot drop them off at the local mechanic for a tune-up or go to the market and purchase a new one.

Your body is the house you and God live in while you are here on earth. It also houses your spirit and your soul. It is amazing to me how we sometimes disrespect something so important. I urge you to use common sense—sleep an adequate number of hours at night, eat the right amounts of good quality, healthy foods, find a way to get plenty of exercise, and laugh a lot because it relieves stress. I also urge you to make adjustments in your schedule so you have some margin in your life and don't feel you must hurry constantly. As I said, your body is not only the temple of your spirit and soul, the house they dwell in while you are on this earth; it is God's home as well. The Bible tells us our body is the temple of the Holy Spirit—He dwells in those who believe in Him (see 1 Corinthians 6:19). Mistreating God's home certainly is not spiritual! God wants us set apart for His use, sanctified—spirit, soul, and body. "Now may the God of peace Himself sanctify you entirely; and may your spirit and soul and body be preserved complete, without blame at the coming of our Lord Jesus Christ" (1 Thessalonians 5:23 NASB).

> Your body is not only the temple of your spirit and soul, the house they dwell in while you are on this earth; it is God's home as well.

Our bodies are our God-given instruments for experiencing life on earth and for doing good works. If we let our bodies become shabby or sick, it will be a constant distraction. To do the work we were meant to do, we need to keep our bodies in shape to allow us to operate most effectively for Him.

Feeling tired and sick most of the time deteriorates the quality of life. Everything becomes more of an effort, and just getting through the day seems to be all we can handle. God wants us to be healthy and energetic, but we need to do our part by using wisdom in how we take care of ourselves.

CHAPTER 76

Respecting Your Body

If you went to visit a church and saw it was extremely run-down, what would you think? If you looked around and noticed peeling paint, broken doors, and smudged windows diminishing the amount of light coming through them, you might find the condition of the church distracting, if not disturbing. Instead of contributing to a feeling of peace, the condition of the church might bring on a feeling of uneasiness. If the pastor's church building is his instrument for celebrating the glory of God, yet he doesn't respect the church enough to keep it in good condition, you might be thinking about whether the pastor's character was in as poor condition as the building placed in his charge.

A church building kept in excellent condition speaks of the excellence of God. Presenting ourselves well physically also represents God well. It is important to remind ourselves God does not expect us to be perfect in any area and to guard against falling into the world's trap of expecting ourselves to have the perfect shape and look nearly perfect. We should work with our bodies, whether we are small-framed or large, whatever our basic makeup is, to be in good shape and present ourselves well without becoming obsessive about our appearance.

We want to keep our bodies in good shape to represent the Lord well, but also to allow our tri-part being to operate most effectively for Him. Jesus wants us to enjoy our lives, and that is very difficult if our bodies are run-down. If we are living in bodies we have basically ignored, experiencing God's presence and His joy and peace in them is about as easy as it would be sitting in the dilapidated church building described in the previous illustration. It is obvious today many people in society are not taking care of themselves. Anyone can see in the way people look and carry themselves, they clearly feel terrible. We simply cannot look our best if we don't feel our best! How we feel will show up somewhere—in our body language, a dull look in our eyes, sullenness of skin color, and so on. We often put ourselves at the bottom of the list of what we take care of, and it adversely affects every other area of our lives. Many people actually hate their bodies.

We often put ourselves at the bottom of the list of what we take care of, and it adversely affects every other area of our lives.

I recently interviewed a doctor on my television program who wrote a book titled *Making Peace with Your Thighs*. She explained how the image presented today by society regarding how we should look is driving people to be dissatisfied with their bodies and even hate them. How can we be comfortable living in a body we hate?

I believe we should take what God has given us to work with and do the best we can with it. Everything about your body may not be exactly as you would like it, but don't despise your body. I have baby-fine hair that is a little difficult to manage, but it won't do me any good to want someone else's hair or hate mine. I have learned to deal with it and do the best I can. You might not like your thighs, your nose, your feet, or some other part of your body, but I encourage you to not focus on the one or two things that are less than desirable. Instead focus on living for God and glorifying Him in your body.

CHAPTER 77

Willpower or God's Power?

When we begin to see things that need to change in us and our lives, it is tempting to think we can change by sheer willpower, but we need more than that. You are familiar with willpower. Willpower makes us not eat the chocolate fudge sundae sitting in front of us, even though every cell of our bodies is screaming for us to dig in. Willpower is that thing CEOs and professional athletes tell us they used to make it to the top. Willpower is what makes you get up and go jogging early every morning.

Willpower sure sounds like a great thing. We are led to believe that we have enough of it to fight off every temptation that comes our way. And sometimes we do have enough. But let me tell you a little secret about willpower. Willpower is your best friend when things are going well, but it's the first friend to check out when you get weary. Willpower peers out Saturday morning at rain and forty-degree temperatures and says, "I'm staying home today!" The problem is willpower is closely aligned with reason, and reason is *always* open to being "reasoned" with, to being talked out of things. "You're right," it says. "Too yucky out for jogging. Sure, you'll go twice tomorrow." Or: "Sure, finish the last piece of pie now so you don't have to put the plate back in the fridge, and then you'll eat a really small dinner tonight. Makes sense!" Reason is always willing to risk the slippery slope leading to failure.

I have found that if I really don't want to do a thing, my mind gives me plenty of reasons why I don't have to. My emotion even joins in, saying, "I agree because I don't feel like doing it," but it is never enough to bring you across the finish line. We live not by our might or power but by God's Spirit (see Zechariah 4:6). Now, what happens if, instead of turning first to willpower in your time of need, you turn to God instead? God releases His power into your willpower and energizes it to bring you across the finish line. Willpower does not get the credit for our success; God does. Jesus said in John 15:5, "Apart from Me... you can do nothing." This is one of the most important and most difficult lessons we must learn if we want to enjoy the life Jesus died to give us. When we go to anything or anyone before God, He is insulted and is obligated to let us fail so we will realize "unless the LORD builds the house, they labor in vain who build it" (Psalm 127:1 NASB).

We must learn to let God do the heavy lifting. Let Him supply the ability to energize our choice. We can choose to exercise or stop overeating, but our choice alone is not enough for complete victory. As I said previously, willpower and determination will get us started, but have been known to quit in the middle and leave us stranded. God never quits in the middle.

> Willpower and determination will get us started, but have been known to quit in the middle and leave us stranded. God never quits in the middle.

There are some people in the world who claim to be self-made successes, but if we follow their lives all the way through, there may be some area of life in which they fall apart. God has not created us to function well without Him, and the sooner we learn that the better off we will be.

Start by asking God to get involved, then continue with God and finish with God. What should we do when the burdens in life seem too heavy? Jesus said, "Come to Me." He will give rest to the weary and burdened (Matthew 11:28).

CHAPTER 78

Receive God's Love

Above all, we need to concentrate on receiving the gift God offers to us every day—His love. His love heals all our wounds and hurts and makes us whole. Once we know how much God loves us, we can begin to love ourselves in a balanced way and then we in turn get to pass it on to others. Receiving God's love is an important step, because we cannot love others without it. We cannot give away what we do not have.

As we begin our new lives in God, we have much to learn and always remembering God loves us will help us receive His correction as a good thing. Love is the greatest gift that can be given, and it is offered to each of us every day, yet few of us have the faith to accept it.

Nothing frustrates me more than people who don't know how to accept gifts. It's a joy to express my love or appreciation to someone by giving them a gift I know they'll like. But if the response is, "No, no, I can't accept that," or "Really, you shouldn't have," or "No, take it back," that drains all the joy out of it. It becomes downright embarrassing if you have to force a gift on someone. You can even begin to wonder if you should have offered the gift at all.

Those who are uncomfortable getting gifts usually have some deep-seated insecurity that prevents them from accepting others' kindness. We often respond the same way to God's free gift of love. Because we have low self-esteem and deep-seated insecurities, we cannot imagine that a perfect God could love an imperfect us. That attitude can prevent us from receiving what God is offering. I must admit I don't know *why* God loves me and wants to have an intimate relationship with me, but His Word says He does and I accept it by faith. Being willing to do that has changed my life, and it will change yours too.

God wants to do many things for each of us. He has gifts prepared for us that we will be unwrapping the rest of our lives. The Bible says, "What eye has not seen and ear has not heard and has not entered into the heart of man, [all that] God has prepared (made and keeps ready) for those who love Him (1 Corinthians 2:9).

Receiving is an action. It isn't passive. You must make the decision to reach out and grab it. Think of a wide receiver catching a pass in football. He isn't called the *wide target*. He doesn't just stand there and wait for the quarterback to stick the ball in his hand. No, he *wants* that ball. He goes after it like a dog after a bone. He'll do anything to get it.

That's how you need to be toward receiving God's love. Be passionate about it. Go after it. Study God's love. Meditate on it. As you seek it eagerly, you will receive a revelation deep in your heart that will be life changing. Learn how to receive God's great gift of love every day and how to give it to others.

For years I desperately wanted to be a good Christian, to give my love to others and have them love me back to help fill the emptiness I felt inside. Yet it never quite worked. I couldn't understand why, and I became frustrated with myself and others. Why was I unable to walk in love? Why weren't people giving me the love I needed? Then I finally realized I had never received God's love—never reached for it. I never liked myself, always feeling unworthy of any gift, much less one as immense as God's love! I made the commitment, opened my heart, and let God rush in with His healing love. Then and only then was I able to love myself, to walk in and enjoy His perfect love, and to give my love to Him and others.

All we have to do is open our hearts and make the decision to receive it. If we never lose sight of God's amazing love, we will be able to enjoy our journey with Him. As God convicts us of things that need to change we set goals for ourselves.

If your goal is to lose fifty pounds and you lose two pounds the first week, should you get discouraged because you are forty-eight pounds heavier than you want to be? No. You say, "Hallelujah, what a great week!" and continue with your plan. Think about your successes rather than your failures. Maybe you ate a little too much today, but the good news is you didn't eat as much as you used to before beginning your new journey toward lifetime health and wholeness. Perhaps you intended to walk thirty minutes but got started late and could only do twenty minutes. Don't feel that you are a failure and should have done better; remember when you did not exercise at all and be happy for your progress. Having this positive attitude toward your progress will breed more progress.

What matters is not where you are, or how far away your destination is, but the direction you are headed. Be proud of *today*. Live one day at a time. Don't look at how far you have to go; look at how far you have come. As Jesus said, "Do not worry about tomorrow, for tomorrow will worry about itself. Each day has enough trouble of its own" (Matthew 6:34 NIV). Do everything you can to make the day a success, and when it is, allow yourself some deep satisfaction in the evening.

What matters is not where you are, or how far away your destination is, but the direction you are headed.

Concentrate on making right choices. Every right choice is one more step toward your destination. Be excited that you are heading in the right direction. It is right to feel good about your progress, rather than bad about how far you still have to go.

The Bible tells us in Ephesians 6 to put on the helmet of salvation, meaning we are to be full of hope and expectation. Learn to be positive about everything. Now that you have begun a new life in Christ, one of the benefits is you can think about everything in a new way. The more you renew your mind and learn to think like God does, the more you will enjoy His good plan for you (see Romans 12:2).

CHAPTER 79

Curb Your Spiritual Hunger

There are some things in life we can't control, and some of those things bring us pain. Illness or injury brings physical pain. Other people can say or do cruel things that cause us emotional pain. And sometimes it doesn't take people at all; circumstances can deal us a bad hand and cause a lot of pain and suffering. Not all of these events are necessarily traumatic. Lots of small hurts in our lives can add up to a general state of sadness or low-grade despair. Sometimes the simple lack of stimulation or loved ones in our lives can contribute to boredom and loneliness, which can be some of the hardest emotional suffering to endure.

Wouldn't it be nice if we could control the people and circumstances in our lives and avoid pain entirely? It's a natural wish; nobody likes pain. Unfortunately, none of us have that control. We all have to live the life we have, and through a personal relationship with Jesus Christ we can enjoy our lives whether our circumstances suit us or not.

Even if we can't control all of our circumstances, one thing we do have control over is our attitude. What is your attitude toward food? Do you give it a place of importance that is out of balance? Do you live to eat or eat to live? We can control what we put into our bodies.

I am sure you don't need me to convince you of the dangers of smoking, or the terrible cost of addiction to drugs and alcohol. We're all aware that such substances are pleasure shortcuts. They are actually a way of avoiding the real issues that need to be dealt with.

When you don't have inner contentment, it becomes all too easy to go for the quick rush of pleasure provided by these vices—even if such pleasure is short-lived and comes with the chronic pain, suffering, and illness of addiction.

But people are less aware that food can play the same role. If I'm feeling down and I eat a candy bar, I feel better for a moment. Not long—the good sensation lasts only a fleeting instant after I swallow it—but fortunately there's another candy bar after that one. And another after that. And even if the candy runs out and my depression returns, there's that pint of ice cream in the fridge for just such emergencies. When the ice cream is gone, there is the chocolate cake or the pie. When we turn to food for comfort, we establish a pattern that is unhealthy and even dangerous—and still leaves us without the comfort we seek.

Food addiction is easy, because food doesn't come with the same stigmas as drugs or alcohol. Unlike those vices, food has a legitimate—even essential—role in health. Only when it slips into overuse does it become a problem. But it's so easy to get to that point! Food is reliable. Unlike spouses, friends, or great weather, it is *always* there. But that's the problem. Any time we are feeling spiritually empty, whether through sadness, depression, or boredom, it's easy to reach for food to fill that void. Soon, we are mistaking spiritual hunger for physical hunger, and food becomes the immediate answer to any drop in well-being.

> The more you try to treat your spiritual longing with food or other feel-good stimuli, the greater your soul's cry for spiritual nourishment will be. The greater your dis-ease will become.

You know where this leads. The more you try to treat your spiritual longing with food or other feel-good stimuli, the greater your soul's cry for spiritual nourishment will be. The greater your dis-ease will become.

You can learn healthy behaviors. For example, reducing stress will help you curb your spiritual hunger. But it is important to learn and practice going to God for what you need instead of using a substitute such as food in trying to ease the pain or find comfort, or instead of being honest before Him about your real need. Fortunately, God is the source of true comfort and is always there when you need Him. Unlike bad food or drugs He doesn't leave you overweight, sick, or lethargic. He freely gives His comfort. The "Father of sympathy (pity and mercy) and the God [Who is the Source] of every comfort (consolation and encouragement), Who comforts (consoles and encourages) us in every trouble" (2 Corinthians 1:3–4) is always there to provide healing of the root cause leading to unhealthy desires in addition to providing the true comfort we need.

When I am hurting, I have learned to run to God first, instead of another person or substance. I'm not saying this is automatic. It took me years to get this straight, and I still sometimes have to remind myself that what I truly need is *spiritual* nourishment. But learning this habit will do more to keep your mind and body sound and your life on an even keel than anything I know. Your spirit needs to be nourished just like your body does. Don't wait until you have a crisis in your life to start feeding it. Nourish yourself spiritually first.

CHAPTER 80

Stay Active

Activity is important not only for weight control and healthy bodies but also for happiness. I believe that inactivity, laziness, and passivity are some of the culprits behind depression and feelings of dissatisfaction. I find that if I am feeling unhappy one of the things that will help is to simply do something. It helps me get my mind off myself and gets my blood flowing. The Bible tells a story of ten virgins waiting for their bridegroom to come. Five were wise and five were foolish. The wise ones stayed alert and spent time getting extra oil for their lamps so they would not go out in case the bridegroom was slow in coming, but the foolish did nothing. They were inactive and lazy, and they did nothing extra so when the bridegroom came they were unprepared and missed their opportunity (see Matthew 25:1–13). You may not be able to change your circumstances, but you can change your habits. Don't let yourself live in ways that allow you to be excessively inactive. Rebel against too much convenience.

Don't let yourself live in ways that allow you to be excessively inactive. Rebel against too much convenience.

To be honest, I think Satan has put one over on us. He has made everything so easy and comfortable and convenient it's killing us. We think we are saving time and effort, but we are really losing strength and energy. Doing work, staying active, is not bad. Don't try to avoid it. We want drive-through service for as many things in life as possible, but the trouble is, *there is no drive-through good health!* Starting today, take steps to make your life a little less convenient and a little more active.

Here are just a few ideas for how to do that:

- Take the stairs. Every time you skip the elevator and walk up a flight, you burn calories, tone some of the muscles you care most about toning, and wake yourself up too.
- Don't waste time looking for the closest parking space. Purposely park so you have to walk a little.
- Walk as much as possible. Think of ways you can get in a little extra walking.
- Don't procrastinate. When you think of a job that needs doing, get up and do it.
- Choose activities that force you to move. Try gardening, sweeping the driveway, dance classes, or mall walking.
- When you watch TV, get up and stretch periodically. Do the same thing at work.
- Sometimes try putting your TV in front of a treadmill and slowly walking while you watch. Go slow enough you aren't distracted. You'll be surprised how quickly it feels natural.
- Keep two five-pound exercise balls or weights in a convenient place where you will see them. Several times a day stop and do a short routine to exercise your upper body. It only takes a minute or two and it loosens up tight muscles.

Try incorporating ways of moving more in your daily life. You'll feel better and be better equipped to serve God and others in your new life!

CHAPTER 81

Power Up!

Whenever the word *exercise* is mentioned, lots of people groan. I'll tell you a secret: I used to groan too! My husband tried to get me to exercise regularly for years and I just hated it. Walking on a treadmill was boring to me, and I always made excuses of being too busy. (We should stop saying, "I don't have the time" regarding exercise, because what we really mean is, "That thing falls too far down on my priority list.")

One day as I was looking at myself in the mirror I sensed God saying in my heart that I needed to get on a good exercise program if I wanted to be strong for what He has called me to do. Dave telling me to exercise seemed to aggravate me, but when God told me it had a different effect on me. I went to a gym and started working with a trainer, and it has been one of the single best things I have ever done in my life. My energy level is amazing, and I lost almost two pant sizes, which would make any woman happy.

Fortunately, gyms don't have a monopoly on exercise. There are thousands of ways to get good exercise, and most don't cost a lot of money, require special equipment, or sidetrack your day. Exercise can be something you look forward to doing if you find what is right for you. Perhaps walking is what you enjoy, or golf or tennis. Maybe you prefer to exercise at home by yourself or would enjoy being in an aerobics class. There are lots of choices, but the bottom line is we need to be active. You might wear a little gadget that measures the steps you take every day. It can become a goal to walk five thousand steps or more each day. I am convinced that God will customize a plan for you if you are willing to do it. In addition to traditional exercise, make an effort to keep your body active in as many small ways as possible.

Sometimes it is a good choice not to use every convenience offered to us. Some forced "inconveniences" are necessary because today we use our bodies so little. We have an abundance of appliances requiring no more than the push of a button to operate. Very few of us have jobs that involve exercise, and most of our leisure activities are spent with our feet up too. This is a new development, and a potentially deadly one. Human beings were made to exercise. Our bodies are fit together with joints because God expected we would be moving a lot.

Human beings were made to exercise. Our bodies are fit together with joints because God expected we would be moving a lot.

We don't read in the Bible about Noah's workout routine or Moses' Pilates session, because everything they did in life involved exercise. Before vehicles, electricity, and machines, everything in the world was run by human power or animal power. If you wanted to get somewhere, you walked. If you needed to bring something with you, you carried it. You did laundry by hand, chopped your own firewood, and ground your own grain. This physically active lifestyle may have been one of the reasons for the incredible longevity of these biblical characters.

The best walker of all may have been Jesus. He routinely walked from His home in Galilee to Jerusalem—a distance of about 120 miles! Over the course of His ministry, He must have walked thousands of miles. In Jesus' day people thought little of walking ten miles. And because they did it all their lives, they had the well-developed bodies to accomplish such long walks with ease. Once when I was in Moscow, I noticed most people were slender. When I asked why, I was informed that most of them had no automobiles and walked everywhere they went.

Even as recently as 1920, people in American towns and cities walked on average nearly two miles to and from work or school, in addition to whatever exercise they got while working. That walk alone burned about two hundred calories per day, which is worth twenty pounds a year in lost weight. When we traded in our daily walk for the convenience of a car, we didn't realize we were getting twenty pounds in the bargain.

The benefit of weight-loss and a better appearance is just the tip of the iceberg. Just a few of the conditions you can help prevent through exercise are heart disease, stroke, diabetes, cancer, Alzheimer's, arthritis, asthma, depression, and gastrointestinal ills. You'll get fewer colds, feel less stress, and look great too. Less fat, more muscle, better tone, straighter posture.

Great things happen when your sneaker hits the pavement and your heart starts pounding.

CHAPTER 82

Eat Fat—The Right Kind

Many nutritionists in the "Low-Fat Wars" of the eighties and nineties told us fat was the enemy. If we could just cut the fat in our diet, they told us, we would lose weight. Soon a horde of low-fat products appeared on store shelves to help us: low-fat cookies, low-fat ice cream, low-fat cheese and chips and frozen dinners. And we snapped them up. We cut the butter, the oil, the meat, and the mayo. We ate every low-fat product known to man. And you know what happened? We got fatter.

The percentage of obese Americans doubled in those two decades from 15 percent to 30 percent. The percentage of overweight children *tripled*. Women now eat 335 more calories per day than they did thirty years ago. How can this be? How can we cut fat and gain weight and even damage our overall health?

> Women now eat 335 more calories per day than they did thirty years ago.

The answer is, the nutritionists who told us to cut fat simply did not know what they were talking about. The whole notion that fat made us fat came from the knowledge that, ounce for ounce, fat has more than twice as many calories as protein or carbohydrates. So replace the fat with an equal weight of something else, and we eat fewer calories, right?

Well, technically, yes. When low-fat diet proponents studied people in the lab, prepared their meals, and measured every calorie they consumed, replacing grams of fat with grams of carbs, it worked just fine. The people lost weight. No matter that they were starving, distracted, and grumpy. That wasn't part of the study. The message went out far and wide: Low-fat, high-carb is your ticket to health and weight loss! Fat is a dirty word!

Unfortunately, things got a little more complicated when real people started trying this diet. Sure, a gram of carbohydrates has fewer calories than a gram of fat, but it turns out that doesn't help much, because the gram of fat is much better at making you feel full. The carbohydrate just makes you want more, so you eat more. The percentage of calories we get from fat dropped from 37 percent to 32, while the percentage of calories from carbohydrates rose from 45 percent to 52.

Other problems came with swapping fat for carbs. Carbohydrates are types of sugar molecules. They don't taste sweet on our tongue because they are too big to fit onto our sugar taste buds, but the body breaks them down into sugar molecules almost instantly. Machines can do it too: corn is a starch that doesn't taste very sweet, but corn syrup is the exact same stuff broken down into little bits, and you know how sweet that is.

No matter what type of carbohydrate you put in your body—french fries or bread or cotton candy—it gets dumped into the blood as glucose for energy. If your muscles happen to be in use at that moment, they'll have plenty of energy. (This is why athletes like to eat some carbohydrates before competing.) If not, well, your body can always convert all that glucose to fat and store it.

Low blood sugar is also known as hypoglycemia. And you know the feeling of low blood sugar: hunger. You feel hungry, your concentration drops, you get grumpy and weak and low in energy. All you can think about is food. So you eat. And if what you eat is mostly carbohydrates, then your blood sugar soars again, you make lots more insulin, and the whole process repeats itself. (Until, of course, your pancreas gets so exhausted from making all the insulin it breaks down and you develop diabetes.) So the net result of the low-fat craze was the consumption of more calories and added health concerns!

So, the issue becomes what kind of fat to eat. Cut back on most red meat and whole-fat dairy, eat more fish and olive oil, and your health risks go down and you will actually consume fewer calories. This is the basis of the now famous Mediterranean Diet, and it's a proven life extender. Switching to a Mediterranean Diet and exercising regularly reduces your risk of heart disease by 80 percent! It's no coincidence this diet is also the basic diet consumed by the people of biblical times: lots of fruits, vegetables, whole grains, and fish, with occasional red meat and poultry and very little dairy (mostly yogurt). It's got quite a track record. So, eat fat—the right kind.

The larger lesson here is the resident truth of the Bible about balance and moderation. Beware of any fad pushing an extreme in any area.

CHAPTER 83

Let Water Do Its Job

Without water you wouldn't have any energy at all, because water is responsible for getting nutrients from your food to your muscles and brain—via blood, which is mostly water. So is the rest of you for that matter! We are all about two-thirds water, and we use water to do everything: to get nutrients to our cells, to cool ourselves, to get rid of waste, and to circulate immune cells through the body. Without enough water, all these systems start to suffer, including metabolism. As you begin to get dehydrated, you get sluggish, because the water isn't there to transfer fuel to your muscles and brain. If you want to keep your metabolism at a high level, it's essential to get enough water each day. In one study in Germany, people's metabolisms immediately rose by 30 percent after drinking two glasses of water and stayed that way for an hour. That's a lot of extra calories burned. And follow this easy rule about water: "If you think of it, drink of it."

You, and all living creatures, must maintain the water content precisely. If it drops below normal, sickness appears. Water is so fundamental to our existence the Bible even compares it to the Word of God. We water our bodies with natural water and our souls with the water of God's Word (see Ephesians 5:26–27). Just as the water of God's Word washes our souls of spiritual filth, so water bathes every one of your cells in life supporting fluid. It's also the fluid *within* your cells. The water

> Water is so fundamental to our existence the Bible even compares it to the Word of God.

routes of your body are the way materials are transported to the cells and the way waste is removed from the cells, just as the waters of the United States were the main transportation routes before the automobile. Without water, energy can't get from your food to your muscles and brain, waste can't get cleansed, kidneys can't function, and the immune system can't circulate. You can't cool yourself either; those little water droplets that get pushed out through the skin as sweat are your main means for dumping excess heat. You can lose a quart of water through sweat if you exercise hard for an hour. If you want your cells to function at their peak—and everything we do or think depends on the functioning of our cells—you need to provide your body with enough water to do its job.

You can go on a hunger strike for a month and suffer no problems worse than a loose wardrobe, but go on a water strike for more than a day and the consequences are severe. Serious dehydration begins with nausea, dizziness, and confusion and leads to muscle cramps, kidney failure, and death.

Even low-grade dehydration has important consequences. When the water level in your body drops, your blood has more trouble getting fuel and other nutrients to your cells, so your energy level drops. Your brain can't run at full power either. You may not even realize you're thirsty, but the evidence is there: fatigue, grumpiness, and weak concentration. If this sounds like you every afternoon, then you are probably not getting enough water. And if you try to fix the fatigue with coffee or cola, even worse: You burn up your remaining energy even faster and are left even more dehydrated by the coffee, which is a diuretic. You'd be surprised how many afternoon slumps can be solved by water.

Let your low-level dehydration go on for too long and you suffer even more. Dry, itchy eyes, dry skin that doesn't "snap back" when pulled, constipation, and kidney stones. Other long-term effects can be even more insidious. A friend's father was showing signs of Alzheimer's disease: confusion, forgetfulness, and so on. My friend is a man of prayer, and he asked God to show him how he might help his father. It came to him that his father never drank water. He claimed he didn't like the taste. So my friend convinced his dad to start drinking water, and sure enough the signs of Alzheimer's disappeared. This does not mean water can cure Alzheimer's disease. It means chronic dehydration can be one cause of Alzheimer's-like symptoms.

Don't rely on thirst to tell you when you need more water. Thirst isn't always reliable, especially in the elderly. You get used to feeling all sorts of ways, some of them bad. Don't get so used to being thirsty you stop noticing. An employee of mine switched from other drinks to water throughout the day and was amazed by how much better she felt. "If a person drinks more water, can it make her thirsty?" she asked. After she started drinking the water, she felt thirst more often. Her body was crying out for more, more, and more water! Give someone a taste of freedom, and he wants more. Give your thirsty body a taste of good, clean water, and suddenly it realizes what it's been missing, and the thirst alarm goes off.

CHAPTER 84

Casual Eating

See if any of this sounds familiar. Every time you pull a snack out of the refrigerator for your children, you pop a little in your mouth. Half a piece of cheese, one slice of ham, or a spoonful of peanut butter. You have no intention of eating the cake you bake, but you lick the batter bowl and the icing knife clean. You get a muffin every day at Starbucks, but throw out half of it to "save calories." You don't order dessert because you're on a diet, but you ask your husband for several bites of his.

The calories in casual, mindless eating add up. I know a woman who drank a glass of milk every night before bed for years. She didn't need that milk; she had just become used to it. She decided to make herself break the habit and lost twelve pounds.

I changed my mindless eating habits to mindful ones by making the commitment to myself that every piece of food I put in my mouth would be a conscious decision. This is harder than it sounds. The way to begin is by paying attention to how many items you are tempted to put in your mouth only because the food is there.

Few of us can do it by willpower alone. We need to call on God to help us be mindful at all times. But here are a few tips helpful for breaking the casual, mindless eating habit:

- Pay attention to how you feel after you eat junk food.
- Pay attention to how you feel after you eat too much.
- Break the habit of snacking while you work or watch TV.
- Eat slowly.

- Turn off the "Bargain Detector": you don't need to buy and eat something because it's a good deal.
- Don't eat something just because someone fixed it for you and *they* want you to eat it.
- Only eat when you are truly hungry and not just because you happen to see some food.

Mindful eating is as important to looking and feeling great as eating the right foods.

We must keep our guard up against this constant whisper to eat, eat, eat. Mindful eating is as important to looking and feeling great as eating the right foods.

CHAPTER 85

Steer Clear of Cortisol

Stress is simply anything that occurs that requires us to react. Our body responds by sending hormones like adrenaline and cortisol through the blood to improve our performance level. Our breathing and heart rate increase, which means more fuel for the muscles and brain. We think faster, react quicker, and have extra strength. This is great, if the stressor is infrequent and if we have some outlet for reacting: running, delivering a sensational performance on stage, or some other way of being active. However, all too often in the modern world we have no physical outlet for the stress. Our boss yells at us in a meeting, we have a fight with our spouse, and we can do nothing but sit there, hormones surging, arteries taking a beating, blood supercharged with oxygen, all bottled up. Constant stress can hand you a quick ticket to the grave. Stick your car in neutral in your driveway, press the gas pedal to the floor, and see how long it takes for your engine to overheat.

> When we experience stress the best thing we can do is what our bodies are screaming at us to do anyway: move!

When we experience stress (and let's face it, most of us deal with it every day) the best thing we can do is what our bodies are screaming at us to do anyway: move! Exercise is the best stress-reducer known to man. It burns up that extra adrenaline and gets our bodies back to a relaxed state, which means you can spend your night sleeping instead of seething. Prayer is the other great stress reliever. Taking your problems to God and trusting Him for answers, protection, and provision replaces pressure with peace.

CHAPTER 86

Make It Easy

Most human beings want everything fast, but God is not in a hurry. He is in this with you for the long haul. He will deliver you from all your bondages little by little. It takes a long time to get our lives into a mess, and it will take some time to see things turned around. Don't be too hard on yourself, especially in the beginning. You have a lot to learn and absorb.

The biggest favor you can do yourself is to not have unrealistic expectations or you will probably end up discouraged. People who try to fix everything that is wrong in one week often give up. Remember, these changes are supposed to last a lifetime.

I have found the secret to success in any long-term project is to make it as easy as possible. You don't need to push yourself to the limit every day of your life unless you're training for the Olympics. You will improve simply by doing something regularly. For most of us, the rewards have to clearly outweigh the inconvenience. All you care about is the outcome, and you don't get extra points for toughness or extreme willpower, so don't make things extra hard on yourself.

I am not saying a new program will always be easy, because it won't. Breaking old bad habits and making new good ones usually present challenges. You will definitely have to resist the temptation to give up at times and be willing to press on during those times when your progress isn't going as fast as you would like. Keeping your commitment to yourself to spend time shopping for and preparing right food items to eat and beginning to exercise regularly will take effort. I am saying you can make it as easy on yourself as possible.

You can do a number of things to make your new lifestyle a relatively painless adjustment. In fact, it pays to start thinking early about the context in which you'll be introducing your new habits. If you are going to start walking a mile a day, try to pick a time when you won't feel pressure not to do it. Arranging your life so your new healthy habits fit right in is a key to long-term commitment. Don't tackle so many things at once that you feel overwhelmed and give up after a short period of time.

Arranging your life so your new healthy habits fit right in is a key to long-term commitment.

What ways can you introduce positive reinforcement into your plan? What ways can you remove temptation to fail? Are there people you can team up with who can help support your goals? Could you plan vacations that focus on health and fitness? Or on relaxation and spiritual refreshment? If we get serious about it, there are innumerable ways most of us can tinker with our lives to help make success easier than failure. You can succeed. I believe you are on your way to great things.

The key to implementing any plan is to take small steps.

Walking a mile takes about two thousand steps. There are no other options or shortcuts. And every one of those steps is a tiny success that brings you closer to your goal. The same is true of any other big goal you reach by breaking the final goal into smaller, doable steps. Plan short-term goals to have something to aim for.

Here are five ways to make success easy:

1) Laugh at setbacks. You will have setbacks. That's part of life. One of the big differences between successful and unsuccessful people is not whether they have setbacks, or even the frequency of their setbacks, but how they respond to them. Successful people are able to have a setback and try again. Having a bad day does not mean you have to have a bad life.

2) Make it convenient. If you are a busy person—and who isn't?—you will have to find ways to fit your program into your schedule.
3) Find exercise and types of foods you like. Making yourself do something you hate won't last very long.
4) Set realistic goals.
5) Reward yourself. When you lay out your short-term and long-term goals, go ahead and jot down some appropriate rewards for yourself with it.

Celebration can be a big part of this. Celebrations and parties help give structure to your journey and let you reflect on what you've accomplished. They also let your friends and family know how important your new goals are to you—and receiving their support can make all the difference.

CHAPTER 87

Put the Tools to Work

It would be so easy had God not given us free will. We could wander through the days like robots, eating the fruit that falls into our hands and waiting for something to happen to us next. But He did give us free will, which gives us tremendous responsibility but also the possibility of total joy and fulfillment.

God will give you all the tools you need on earth to reach spiritual completion. But it is up to you to take up those tools and put them to work restoring your health and respecting the body He gave you. He will help you and make it as easy on you as possible, but He won't do the work for you. The work is an essential part of the fulfillment, an essential part of the process of freeing your soul from bondage. When you are in the depths of self-pity, knowing you are the one who must make right choices can feel like a pressure and responsibility you just don't want; but once you make the commitment to maintaining your body and soul as you should to be a person of excellence and power, you discover that free will is your most valuable possession.

> God will give you all the tools you need on earth to reach spiritual completion. But it is up to you to take up those tools and put them to work.

That is why you must avoid self-pity at all costs. Self-pity is an emotion that feeds on itself and steals your power. You need power to become the person you were meant to be, and you cannot be pitiful and powerful at the same time. I had a major problem with self-pity in my earlier years, and not until I stopped feeling sorry for myself did I start making progress.

We feel better about ourselves when we approach life boldly, ready to be accountable and responsible. You don't have to hide from anything. You can do whatever you need to do in life. You can look healthy and attractive. You can feel great inside and out. You can live a life that keeps you fit and happy and productive for God into old age. It is all up to you. Through God, you are ready for anything. Confront your life head on and never turn back!

When it comes to taking responsibility for your own life, there is no wiggle room. The time has come to be very honest with yourself and with God. You either do what is right or you don't! Make the decision to use everything you have learned about walking with God to break old habits and be transformed. When you have a moment of privacy, take a deep breath, clear your head, and repeat this phrase:

"I am responsible for my own life. No one can take charge of it but me. If I am unhappy or unhealthy, I know I have the power to change. I have all the help and knowledge I need, and with God's hand today I will start becoming the person of excellence I have always known I could be."

Blessings on you for the exciting and wondrous journey you are taking.

CHAPTER 88

God Restores Us Soul and Body

Over the years I have learned how to take care of myself; and most of all I have learned that I can have a lifetime of health for my body and soul. I believe good health for the whole person requires a solid faith in God through Jesus Christ. He helped me through all the rough years and He restored me. God showed me what to do and led me to make positive changes. Sometimes it took me a long time to fully obey, but I can say from experience, God's ways work. His Word is filled with guidelines for good health; any person who follows them will experience good results.

> I believe good health for the whole person requires a solid faith in God through Jesus Christ.

I have been in some deep, dark places where I could see no light at all. I started my life in such a place. I know how hopeless it can seem. My home life when I was young was extraordinarily dysfunctional. I began to feel the effects of it in my body by the time I was a teenager. The first trouble I remember was constipation and stomach pains. I went to the doctor, who told me I had a spastic colon. Only years later did I learn that disorder is usually caused by excessive tension, nervousness, and stress. Remember, any time the body cannot relax, that state of "dis-ease" promotes disease.

By the time I was thirty-six I began having more serious symptoms in my body. I got sick for four months straight. I felt so bad most of the time I could hardly get off the couch. I realize now it was because my body was already breaking down due to the years of stress. Later I started having hormone imbalances. My monthly periods were too frequent and excessive. I took shots of estrogen every ten days to be able to function. Eventually I had a hysterectomy, which immediately plunged me into the "change of life."

In 1989 I was diagnosed with breast cancer. The tumor was fast-growing and estrogen-dependent, which not only meant I needed immediate surgery but also that I could no longer take hormone-replacement therapy while going through early menopause. I had surgery and endured several more years of sheer misery because my hormonal system was such a mess. As you might imagine, with this and a few other related health problems, I was a wreck.

Despite all of this I continued my work in the ministry. I traveled, taught God's Word, stood in faith for my own healing, and often wondered how I could go on much longer. I worked hard, but I did not enjoy *anything.*

Eventually I started reading books on nutrition and exercise. I firmly believe God led me to them. I began to realize that eating right and physical activity had to be a way of life. Going on fad diets to lose some weight, only to return to bad habits and gain it back, was getting me nowhere. I was tired of that cycle. I imagine many of you are also.

The books I read at that time did not include information on stress. Back then, few scientists understood the strength of the mind-body connection like they do today. Plenty of the doctors I saw (and I was always seeing doctors) did tell me that I was under extreme stress and desperately needed to make some lifestyle changes. I knew I couldn't just take a year off to recover. We had a large staff at our ministry and I felt they all depended on me. After all, if I did not do my part, then nobody got a paycheck. When people who loved me tried to tell me I needed to stop working so hard, I just told them they did not understand my calling.

I was helping everyone else but not taking the time to help myself. I was a workaholic. Even though this all seemed overwhelming and insurmountable, God taught me about living a balanced life, and through that knowledge He delivered me from poor health.

I can truthfully say that I feel better physically, mentally, emotionally, and spiritually than I ever have in my life. That's a big claim! I live every day passionately, and what a breathtaking change that is. Too many of us get trapped in a rut of negative thinking, believing our healthiest days are behind us and that we will simply get more out of shape, sicker, and less energetic as we age. I'm living proof that's not so! These are my best days. I have energy and contentment as I've never known, a fierce faith, and I fully expect to live out my life in health and grace. No matter your age or condition, you can do the same. We have a promise from God that we can still be very productive in old age. If you haven't done so already, begin today making the right choices to live a healthy and productive lifestyle for all your life.

CONCLUSION

Trust God

My prayer as I finish this book is that it will be an invigorating launch point for your new life of faith in Christ. You may not understand all the material I have covered but I hope you will keep this resource handy and allow its instruction to continue to encourage and strengthen you for years to come. As I've said many times, your transformation into the image of Jesus is a process that will not be complete until we see him face-to-face, so be sure you don't get discouraged if your progress seems slow. Keep taking steps of faith each day holding to God's Word, seeking His will, and living in His ways, and you will keep moving toward the abundant life He's promised!

I want to encourage you to also pursue an active relationship with a local church. It is important to be with people who want to serve God like you do. You need to find a church that feels like home to you, so even if it takes a while just keep looking. Worshiping God and studying His Word with others is a vital part of growing in God. And be sure you find a church that believes in and teaches the Bible as the complete and flawless Word of God. Attend regularly, learn incessantly, and give of your time and resources. If you've not been baptized, I recommend you do that as soon as possible in obedience to God's Word. It is an outward sign of your inward decision to follow Christ.

I urge you seek the power of the Holy Spirit daily, because He is the One Who gives us the help we need to live a successful and fruitful life. Lean on God for everything, because without Him you can do nothing.

If you are anything like I was, you may have tendencies toward selfishness so you must learn to give. Giving is a vital part of the Christian lifestyle that Jesus teaches. Give of all your resources including time, talent, and money. Helping others through giving is one of the best things you can do for yourself. When you help someone else, you actually release joy in your own life.

Each of our lives is a journey and we don't always understand all the things we encounter along the way. Some of the things that happen to us do not seem to be fair, but if we trust God He causes all things to work out for good in the end.

Learning to trust God at all times is the only way we can successfully complete our journey with joy. Trust means we will always have some unanswered questions. We won't mentally understand everything that takes place because God's ways are far above our ways. Although we don't always understand God, we can always trust Him. He is good and only seeks to do what will benefit us in the end.

God wants to be your friend so I encourage you to talk to Him as you would a close friend. Always give Him first place in your life and serve Him with your whole heart. Thank you for allowing me the privilege of sharing God's Word and principles with you.

I pray that you will enjoy every day of your new life!

About the Author

JOYCE MEYER is one of the world's leading practical Bible teachers. A #1 *New York Times* bestselling author, she has written more than seventy inspirational books, including *The Confident Woman, I Dare You,* the entire Battlefield of the Mind family of books, her first venture into fiction with *The Penny,* and many others. She has also released thousands of audio teachings as well as a complete video library. Joyce's *Enjoying Everyday Life®* radio and television programs are broadcast around the world, and she travels extensively conducting conferences. Joyce and her husband, Dave, are the parents of four grown children and make their home in St. Louis, Missouri.

Other Books by Joyce Meyer

New Day, New You Devotional

I Dare You

The Penny

The Power of Simple Prayer

The Everyday Life Bible (hardcover or bonded leather)

The Confident Woman

Look Great, Feel Great

*Battlefield of the Mind**

Battlefield of the Mind Devotional

Battlefield of the Mind for Teens

Battlefield of the Mind for Kids

Approval Addiction

Ending Your Day Right

21 Ways to Finding Peace and Happiness

The Secret Power of Speaking God's Word

Seven Things That Steal Your Joy

Starting Your Day Right

Beauty for Ashes (revised edition)

*Study Guide available for this title.

*How to Hear from God**

Knowing God Intimately

The Power of Forgiveness

The Power of Determination

The Power of Being Positive

The Secrets of Spiritual Power

The Battle Belongs to the Lord

The Secrets to Exceptional Living

Eight Ways to Keep the Devil Under Your Feet

Teenagers Are People Too!

Filled with the Spirit

Celebration of Simplicity

The Joy of Believing Prayer

Never Lose Heart

Being the Person God Made You to Be

A Leader in the Making

"Good Morning, This Is God!" (gift book)

Jesus—Name Above All Names

Making Marriage Work
(previously published as
Help Me—I'm Married!)

Reduce Me to Love

Be Healed in Jesus' Name

How to Succeed at Being Yourself

Weary Warriors, Fainting Saints

*Be Anxious for Nothing**

Straight Talk Omnibus

Don't Dread

Managing Your Emotions

Healing the Brokenhearted

*Me and My Big Mouth!**

Prepare to Prosper

Do It Afraid!

Expect a Move of God in Your Life... Suddenly!

Enjoying Where You Are on the Way to Where You Are Going

A New Way of Living

When, God, When?

Why, God, Why?

The Word, the Name, the Blood

Tell Them I Love Them

Peace

*If Not for the Grace of God**

Joyce Meyer Spanish Titles

Las Siete Cosas Que Te Roban el Gozo
(Seven Things That Steal Your Joy)

Empezando Tu Dia Bien
(Starting Your Day Right)

Books by Dave Meyer

Life Lines

To contact the author:

Joyce Meyer Ministries—U.S. Headquarters
P.O. Box 655
Fenton, MO 63026
USA
(636) 349-0303
www.joycemeyer.org

Joyce Meyer Ministries—Canada
Lambeth Box 1300
London, ON N6P 1T5
Canada
1-800-727-9673

Joyce Meyer Ministries—Australia
Locked Bag 77
Mansfield Delivery Centre
Queensland 4122
Australia
(07) 3349 1200

Joyce Meyer Ministries—England
P.O. Box 1549
Windsor SL4 1GT
United Kingdom
(0) 1753 831102

Joyce Meyer Ministries—South Africa
P.O. Box 5
Cape Town 8000
South Africa
(27) 21-701-1056